COLLABORATE TO CREATE

A GUIDE TO COAUTHORING NONFICTION

MATTY DALRYMPLE

M.L. RONN

WILLIAM KINGSFIELD PUBLISHERS

Matty dedicates this book to my collaborator in life, Wade Walton.

Michael dedicates this book to all of his writing collaborators past, present and future, who inspire him and make him a better writer.

CONTENTS

FOREWORD

I remember sitting in McMichael Science Center at Elon University many years ago for biochemistry class and the professor lecturing about synergistic reactions. This particular reaction is one where the outcome of the whole is greater than the sum of the individual reactants. The beauty of this concept is that it doesn't just apply to chemical reactions. We see this phenomenon—synergy—when people put their minds together in academics, politics, business, and art. Orville and Wilbur Wright changed the way humans travel with their flying machine, and singer-songwriters John Lennon and Paul McCartney arguably changed the direction of music. The bottom line: when two or more people put their heads together something magical can happen.

Matty Dalrymple and Michael La Ronn (M.L. Ronn) have put their heads together in *Collaborate to Create* to help you unlock some of that magic in your next (even if it's your first) coauthored book.

I never dreamed in a million years I'd be involved in a successful coauthor book collaboration, but as you'll learn in *Collaborate to Create*, you simply need to be open to opportunities in unusual places. That opportunity presented itself to me at a photo shoot for a beefcake calendar ... for morticians. Two years later *Mortuary Confidential* was released and propelled my writing career into the stratosphere.

Matty and Michael will break down some of that "magic" and offer a practical roadmap if you're thinking about coauthoring. There are things they cover that I did with my coauthored project such as:

- recognizing opportunities for collaboration in unusual places
- conducting a skills assessment of all involved
- formalizing the writing partnership with a contract

But *Collaborate to Create* also covers things I wish I'd known prior to my coauthoring foray:

- the nuts and bolts: version control of the manuscript, communication best practices, and choosing the best platform (for both authors) in which to write your book
- negotiating content creation
- marketing and promotion tips to maximize the book launch

Collaborate to Create will teach you how to use your current project to leverage your next (solo or coauthored) project. *Mortuary Confidential* led to *Over Our Dead Bodies* and opened the door for multiple solo projects.

Just remember, Irv Robbins thought he was doing okay with a few Snowbird Ice Cream stores in Glendale, California as did Burt Baskin with a few Burton's Ice Cream Stores around Pasadena. It wasn't until the duo paired up that Baskin-Robbins became a household name. Do yourself a favor: take Matty and Michael's advice and you just might be the next Baskin-Robbins at Barnes & Noble.

Todd Harra
Coauthor of *Mortuary Confidential: Undertakers Spill the Dirt* and *Over Our Dead Bodies: Undertakers Lift the Lid.*

INTRODUCTION

We're so glad you've joined us on this exploration of coauthoring nonfiction! We believe that collaboration offers benefits across a whole host of areas, and in *Collaborate to Create: A Guide to Coauthoring Nonfiction*, we will help you understand what a collaborative effort can bring to your writing and publishing efforts, how you and your coauthor can capitalize on the opportunities, and how to avoid the pitfalls that can founder a collaborative project.

What do we find appealing about coauthoring?

Anyone familiar with **Matty**'s nonfiction platform, The Indy Author, is familiar with her love of the nautical metaphor, and as with so many other topics related to the writing craft and the publishing voyage, sailing offers a great metaphor for collaborative work: double-handed sailing teams in competitive racing.

In double-handed sailing, two sailors manage all aspects of the voyage—plotting the course, adjusting the sails, maintaining the craft—on a journey that demands precision, trust, and seamless coordination.

Each sailor brings unique strengths. One might excel at reading the wind and trimming the sails, while the other is a master at plotting the course and maintaining focus under pressure. Success depends on the ability to harmonize distinct roles and communicate effectively, even under the stress of rough seas or unanticipated headwinds. For longer races, one sailor might need to take full responsibility for the craft for a period of time to enable the other to rest.

Like these sailors, coauthors steer their book to the finish line of a journey that neither could have achieved on their own.

Michael sees another metaphor for collaboration in his own life: video games and the concept of "leveling up"—a concept that he used for his author business, Author Level Up.

In the gaming world, to level up means to ascend to a new level where the skills learned at an earlier level help the player navigate the new level's challenges. Players must continue to practice their new skills to move to the next challenge, in a constant state of simultaneously exercising their existing mastery and achieving new levels of mastery.

When two people combine their skills, they can level up much faster, as in two gamers tag-teaming a level in a video game. In the same way two sailors must have precision, trust, and seamless coordination, so too must gamers work together to achieve their goals. Some games are best played solo, but others can only be won through collaboration.

We believe that some goals of a writing and publishing career are more attainable via collaboration than via solo work.

Why Coauthoring ... and Why This Book?

Collaborating on a nonfiction book brings with it so many potential benefits, enabling you to:

- Tap into the knowledge of your coauthor to deepen your knowledge of a topic about which you are already an expert.
- Become an expert in a topic that's new to you.
- Add a book to your portfolio that might never have been created as a solo work.
- Expand your audience to your coauthor's fans and introduce your coauthor to your own fans.
- Earn income from your jointly produced work.
- Lay the foundation of a relationship that can benefit both of you long after the book has been published.

Matty values collaboration because it expands the portfolio of topics on which she can offer courses and workshops and expands her exposure to and reputation within the indie author community she wants to reach.

Michael values collaboration because it moves him toward his goal of building a portfolio of nonfiction that covers every aspect of what it means to be a self-published author in the twenty-first century.

Which of these seem most appealing to you and align most closely with your goals for your author career? What benefits do you anticipate from coauthoring beyond the ones we've listed? (You'll have a chance to capture these at the end of this section.)

Our Coauthoring Experiences

Matty's first collaborative effort was with the book *Taking the Short Tack: Creating Income and Connecting with Readers Using Short Fiction*, which she coauthored with Mark Leslie Lefebvre. Matty, who had indie published some Ann Kinnear Suspense Shorts and was wondering what else she could do with these works, heard Mark make a brief mention on his *Stark Reflections on Writing and Publishing* podcast about the promotion and marketing opportunities that short fiction offers writers. She got in touch with Mark and asked him if he would consider doing a full podcast episode on this topic, which he promptly did. She got in touch with him again, saying that she thought the episode provided the basis of a book and asking if he would be willing to coauthor that book with her. Mark agreed, and *Taking the Short Tack* was born.

What drove Matty to pursue a coauthored book? First, she knew that writing the book with Mark would provide a fantastic opportunity to deepen her understanding of the business side of short fiction, a topic about which Mark is an expert. The idea of gaining experience in a creative approach she had never used before, coauthoring, was appealing. And, frankly, she was enthusiastic about tapping into Mark's reputation and reach in her target audience: fellow indie authors.

Michael's first collaboration was with fiction: writing the bestselling fantasy thriller series *Modern Necromancy* with his friend Justin Sloan. They wrote this series before collaborations were popular and before many of the current tools on the market were created. On the nonfiction front, Michael also coauthored the bestselling nonfiction book *150 Self-Publishing Questions Answered* with Orna Ross, Director of the Alliance of Independent Authors.

The first book Matty and Michael coauthored together, *From Page to Platform: How to Succeed as an Author Speaker*, came about based on a conversation we had over dinner when we were in New York teaching at the Writer's Digest annual conference. We discussed how we had landed the gig, approaches we took in negotiating our speaker agreements, and some of the best (and worst) practices we had developed or seen related to delivering an excellent presentation and engaging our audiences. By the end of that conversation, we knew we had enough valuable information to share with our fellow authors to merit a book.

And this book, *Collaborate to Create: A Guide to Coauthoring Nonfiction*, came about because once we had completed work on *From Page to Platform*, we recognized the value that collaboration on a nonfiction work could bring, realized that we had developed a valuable set of best practices for such work, and knew that others could benefit from hearing about the challenges we faced and how we overcame them.

What We Cover

We define coauthoring as ***an endeavor where multiple authors share the collaborative effort of planning, writing, editing, publishing, marketing, and promoting a new book and are compensated for that work through a sharing of the resulting royalties***. The advice in *Collaborate to Create* could theoretically apply to collaborations involving more than two authors, but each additional collaborator exponentially increases the complexity of the process; **we recommend that especially for a first coauthoring effort, you stick with one other collaborator**.

We assume that **the coauthors will publish the work under both their names**—for example, *Matty Dalrymple and M.L. Ronn*—rather than creating a single pen name under which to publish the book (an approach that is more common for fiction than nonfiction). The creation of a separate pen name introduces logistical and legal complications that are beyond the scope of this book.

Our definition of coauthoring means **we don't address**

works such as anthologies, since although an anthology itself is a new product, the creation of each component part is not collaborative in the same sense that coauthored content is collaborative, and the component works are not new pieces of written IP.

This also means **we don't address ghostwriting**, since although it involves collaboration with another creator (although perhaps not with another author), the ghostwriter generally doesn't share in a book's royalties but receives a flat fee for their service.

And, although some of the best practices of coauthoring are common across both nonfiction and fiction, **we focus on nonfiction in this book**, enabling us to dive deep into advice related specifically to nonfiction as well as to use our own coauthored efforts as examples.

A final note: Much of the advice in this book applies regardless of whether the book will be indie published or traditionally published. For example, the benefits and requirements for coauthoring are largely the same in both situations. There are a few sections—such as negotiating contracts—that apply more specifically to indie-published books, but for purposes of readability, we assume these will be clear and don't call these out specifically.

For Your Consideration

At the end of each section, we include questions for you to answer. How does the information we've shared resonate with you as you navigate the coauthoring process? What actions will you commit to take based on what you've learned? You can capture your responses in the downloadable document available at TheIndyAuthor.com/Collaborate, and these notes will serve as a map for your coauthoring efforts.

For this section ...

- Note three potential benefits of coauthoring that have prompted you to pursue these opportunities.

WHAT DOES COAUTHORING OFFER?

Coauthoring offers a host of opportunities, and we explore the most common benefits in this section, including:

- Learning
- Expanding your portfolio
- Building relationships with fellow creators
- Expanding audience reach
- Earning

Opportunities for Learning

Collaboration enables you to pool your knowledge with another creator. Matty's first coauthoring experience was with *Taking the Short Tack: Creating Income and Connecting with Readers Using Short Fiction* with Mark Lefebvre. Matty had plenty of experience indie publishing her Ann Kinnear Suspense Shorts, but Mark had far more experience with the traditional short fiction market, and that collaboration enabled Matty to expand her knowledge in that area.

Michael's goal in coauthoring is to expand his knowledge

and write books that supplement his knowledge base with perspectives he wouldn't have considered on his own. For example, he would have never considered writing a book on public speaking until he met Matty!

There's nothing like writing about or editing content about a topic to cement your knowledge of it.

Opportunities for Expanding Your Portfolio

Coauthoring can expand your portfolio of work because coauthored books are often books that wouldn't have been written at all if they relied on a solo effort.

The topic of being an author speaker was one Matty had been toying with as a book topic for some time. However, it wasn't until she and Michael happened to fall into a conversation about it when they were presenting at a Writer's Digest conference that it came to fruition. The topic of production, distribution, marketing, and promotion of short fiction was one she was interested in but didn't personally have the experience to fully explore, a gap that was filled when she paired with Mark Lefebvre on *Taking the Short Tack*.

Opportunities for Building Relationships with Fellow Creators

There are plenty of opportunities to build a network of writing colleagues through forums like writers' groups or conferences, but there is no deeper relationship you will build than when you embark on coauthored project.

Successful coauthoring relationships are those where the collaborators share overlapping areas of interest, compatible creative visions, and aligned business goals, so the value of these relationships can be even more significant than with less closely aligned colleagues. Furthermore, navigating challenges together

—whether it's meeting deadlines or refining a plan in face of unexpected circumstances—creates a sense of solidarity. Coauthors become sounding boards for one another, offering advice and encouragement even after the project is complete. A successful coauthoring experience often leads to additional collaborations, whether on more books or other projects.

Opportunities for Expanding Audience Reach

Coauthoring provides an opportunity for each author to introduce their work to their coauthor's fans and followers. One of Matty's goals in coauthoring books with Mark Lefebvre and Michael was the desire to tap into that large intersection of the fans they had attracted in the indie author community and the audience she wanted to reach.

Opportunities for Earning

More content and a larger audience means more potential income, so coauthoring can expand your earnings as well.

Opportunities for Timesaving?

One aspect that each author has to weigh for themselves is whether coauthoring is a timesaver.

Matty once interviewed the coauthor of a thriller series who saw coauthoring as a way to address the challenge of having "more ideas than time." Her process with her coauthor involved one author creating the story outline, the other "putting meat on the bones," and the first making some final refinements. This process was efficient and timesaving because each author focused on the part of the creation process that they were best at. The same could hold true for nonfiction.

Against this, you must weigh the fact that the coordination needed for a collaborative project takes time, so a coauthored project might actually take more hours and stretch over a longer time than a solo project. We're all busy, and we may need to fit in a co-authored project between other endeavors, so don't be surprised if a coauthoring project takes longer—maybe considerably longer—than a solo one.

We don't recommend that you go into a collaborative project expecting it to save time; instead, consider any time-savings benefits you enjoy as an added bonus. As the saying goes ...

If you want to go fast, go alone; if you want to go far, go together.

We believe the benefits of how far you can go to be the true power of collaboration.

For Your Consideration

Consider the following and capture your responses in the downloadable document available at TheIndyAuthor.com/Collaborate. For this section ...

- Note which of the benefits that coauthoring offers—learning, expanding your portfolio, building relationships, expanding audience reach, or earning—most appeals to you and why?

WHAT DOES COAUTHORING REQUIRE?

Embarking on a collaboration is not a decision to take lightly. It's a decision that will have ramifications for you and your partner author for the rest of your careers, and even on your heirs after your death. We advise thinking of it as a creative marriage; consider carefully whether you're willing to step up to the requirements of a successful collaboration, which we explore in this section.

Sharing the Creative Process

For many of us, writing is among the most personal things we do, and our words are the things we may want to protect most ferociously. A collaboration means that you will have someone else reading your unpolished draft material, commenting on it, perhaps even questioning whether some of it merits inclusion in your book. You will be doing the same for your collaborator.

For example, you may write a chapter that you're attached to, but your coauthor might not think it is necessary. Are you willing to take criticism, negotiate, and ultimately make a decision that might mean you don't get everything you want as long as it serves the greater good?

Coauthoring is an exercise in vulnerability and trust, and it is not one to embark on lightly. There will be disagreements, and both you and your coauthor will need to have the openness and emotional intelligence to navigate any issues that arise.

Sharing the Responsibility

On the creative front ...

Are you ready to deliver the work you and your potential collaborator are likely to agree will be your responsibility? The work of each contributor will wax and wane over the course of the project, but imagine yourself at the conclusion of your collaboration—will you be able to look back on the project with confidence that you did your part?

For example, when Matty considered coauthoring a project with Michael, she knew she would be partnering with someone well known in the author community for his prolific output. She didn't expect to be able to generate the same amount of content in the same amount of time as Michael, but she felt confident that over the course of a project with a generous schedule, she would be able to contribute her fair share of material.

On the business front ...

Can you step up to your portion of the work related to everything that comes after the content is drafted: editing, production, distribution, marketing, and promotion, and the project management tasks required to ensure it all runs smoothly?

For example, if you both agree to use your network of contacts to promote the book, can you follow through with that? Can you commit to taking the time to handle your part of the business side of the collaborative work even though you will undoubtedly have other projects—maybe solo projects—demanding your time and attention?

Sharing the Control

Sharing the responsibility of a collaborative project means stepping up to what needs to be done, but as challenging as this can be, its opposite—the need to share control—can be an even greater challenge.

Ceding some control over the writing and publishing processes can be difficult for any author; however, it may be most difficult for indie authors, who are used to calling the shots for their own works and having the buck—and the decisions—stop with them. However, you'll need to be prepared to adjust your expectations if you want to lay the foundation for a successful collaboration. Decisions will need to be negotiated with your coauthor, and it's unlikely, and probably undesirable, for you to always get your own way.

Collaboration always involves sharing responsibility and ceding some control. How willing you are to do that? For example, how comfortable would you feel about a situation where ...

- You feel the need to settle on a cover design you don't love?
- You are asked to accommodate a distributor you've never used before?
- You have to negotiate the tricky exclusive-or-wide decision?
- You risk seeing social media posts promoting your book that don't feel brand-right?
- You are asked to consider a price discount when the book is selling well at full price?

- You need to discuss with another creator decisions like expansion into translations?

Your answers to these questions are a good indicator of whether the sharing of control required by coauthoring will be a natural fit for you or more of a challenge.

But even if you felt uncomfortable as you read through those questions, don't count yourself out of the coauthoring game—we will be offering advice throughout this book for how to negotiate this tricky process, and even enjoy the journey!

Not for Everyone … or for Every Book

We are obviously proponents of the benefits of coauthoring, but we recognize that it's not for everyone, or for every circumstance.

If you're an introvert, you might find the idea of negotiating the interpersonal aspects of a collaboration mentally exhausting or even intimidating. If you work best if you have the ability to move from one project to another as inspiration strikes you, that can be problematic when working with a partner who expects you to provide content on specific topics within specific time-frames. If you're juggling many different life responsibilities, the demands of a coauthored project might not be compatible with that.

In some cases, going solo is the best option. If you're an indie author, it will provide you with the greatest control over every aspect of the work. If maximizing your income is a key goal for your author career, solo works might be a better way to achieve that. Ultimately you need to decide how much of your writing time you will devote to collaborative versus solo work.

But remember, you can make the decision about whether or not to collaborate for each piece of work, not for your author career as a whole. Few authors collaborate exclusively. Michael divides his time among projects based on impact and priority. Matty chose to write *The Indy Author's Guide to Podcasting for Authors* solo because it was based on her own experience with The Indy Author Podcast and as a guest on others' podcasts.

But the benefits of collaborative work can extend to all of an author's works; many writers find that collaborations add value and richness to their solo works. For example, you may find that constructive criticism from your coauthor can be applied to your solo writing. Michael discovered that he tends to overcomplicate concepts. Matty's feedback helped him think about presenting his arguments differently and more effectively in his next solo works.

There are a lot of factors to consider when making this decision to collaborate; don't take it lightly.

But also don't be cynical or distrustful. Assuming that you pick the right collaborator—which our advice will help you do—you'll be able to enjoy all the benefits we cover in the section "What Does Coauthoring Offer?" And this book will help you through the inevitable bumps you'll encounter along the way.

For Your Consideration

Consider the following and capture your responses in the downloadable document available at TheIndyAuthor.com/Collaborate. For this section ...

Read through the following lists of characteristics and note your reaction to each description. This will give you an indicator if coauthoring will be a natural fit for you or whether it will be more of a challenge.

If these scenarios resonate with you ...

- I'm motivated by deadlines.

- I enjoy tossing around ideas related to content with fellow creators.
- There are specific parts of the writing and publishing process that I enjoy more / am better at.
- If I'm onstage, I'm happy to share the spotlight with others.
- I'm pretty easygoing; there is rarely a hill I'm willing to die on.

… then coauthoring will likely be a natural fit for you. If these scenarios resonate with you …

- I value flexibility of schedule.
- I have a clear idea of what I want to create, and how I want to create it.
- I enjoy / am comfortable with all aspects of the writing and publishing process.
- If I'm onstage, I consider it my responsibility to hold the audience's attention.
- If I feel a decision has a clear right and wrong answer, I stick to my guns.

… then coauthoring may be more of a challenge for you—but not an insurmountable one!

FINDING THE OPPORTUNITIES

I've always said that the future of publishing is going to be more collaborative than ever before. And I'm excited that we got to do this collaboration. I mean, think about how we connected— through common interests and common goals and common aspirations as writers, as indie authors.

—Mark Leslie Lefebvre, Episode 14 of *The Indy Author Podcast* "Collaborating on *Taking the Short Tack: Creating Income and Connecting with Readers Using Short Fiction*"

There are as many stories of how a coauthored project came about as there are coauthored projects, but one of the most effective ways to discover coauthoring opportunities is by being an active participant in the communities related to your topic of interest. For many of us, these will be the writing and publishing communities.

Coauthoring partnerships often begin with a conversation.

Perhaps you and another writer discover a mutual interest during a panel discussion or workshop, or maybe a casual chat with a publisher or editor at an industry conference introduces you to someone who complements your strengths. These serendipitous moments of connection are far more likely to happen when you're engaged and visible in the community.

Be open to discussing your expertise and interests. Sometimes, just talking about what excites you can inspire a collaboration, especially when the event is organized around a theme, such as a genre-specific writers' conference. In online communities, actively contribute to discussions to make yourself known.

Don't limit your participation only to writing- and publishing-related communities. Opportunities can arise out of other commonalities such as professional connections, shared hobbies, or interest in certain causes. We especially enjoy this story from author Todd Harra:

The first book I had commercial success with, Mortuary Confidential, was a coauthored project, and it came about in a very unusual way.

There was a man who had started a breast cancer foundation to provide practical support for women undergoing treatment, helping them with things like groceries, childcare, and plane tickets when they needed to travel for specialized care. He also owned a funeral home in Long Beach, California, and to fund his charity, he created a morticians' calendar, similar to the firefighters' calendars that had become popular.

In 2008, I tried out for the calendar, was accepted, and went out to Long Beach for the photo shoot. While I was there, he and I got to talking, and I mentioned that I was a writer. That's when he told me he had an idea for another stream of income for his foundation: a book of mortician stories. He had already hired a ghostwriter, but things hadn't worked out. He asked if I'd be interested in taking on the project.

I could see it was a fantastic idea, but instead of accepting a ghostwriter role, I made him a counteroffer: I would write the book on spec and get my name on the cover in exchange for 50/50 split of the proceeds. He agreed.

That's how Mortuary Confidential came to be. We've sold over 100,000 copies of that book, so my gut feeling was right—the response exceeded everyone's expectations.

If there's one takeaway from this experience, it's that you never know where you're going to find a coauthor or an idea for a book. Be open to finding opportunities in unusual situations and recognize when something has potential. Sometimes, a simple conversation can lead to an unexpected writing project.

In this case, Todd found the opportunity to coauthor *Mortuary Confidential* because he was involved in another fund-raising effort masterminded by the man who would become his collaborator. But most authors will find their coauthoring opportunities by being active members of the writing and publishing communities.

For Your Consideration

Consider the following and capture your responses in the downloadable document available at TheIndyAuthor.com/Collaborate. For this section …

- Where might you find opportunities for collaboration?

EXPLORING THE OPPORTUNITY

Any project involving co-creation should be entered into with consideration; coauthoring a book project deserves special attention because you will be working closely with your collaborator for months or even years and will be living with the consequences—good and bad—of that collaboration for years if not decades. A collaboration is like a creative marriage and should be entered into with (almost) the same level of care.

We have listed the considerations for exploring an opportunity in this section in rough priority order. For example, we recommend that you assess your potential collaborator's professional standing before you consider the mechanism to be used for dividing royalties, because the royalty-splitting tool won't make much difference if your collaborator turns out to be a swindler.

Conducting Your Own Assessment

First, consider the assessment you need to do on your own, before you enter into conversation with your potential coauthor.

Assess for Bandwidth

Before anything else, consider whether you have the mental, emotional, and chronological bandwidth for a new project. As experienced coauthor Nicholas Harvey says:

If you're a full-time author (especially indies), then your dance card is almost certainly full, so thinking you'll squeeze in 2,000 words on the collab project every week or two is great in theory but often tougher to do in practice. As these things always go, the manuscript lands back in your lap just as you've fallen behind on your next scheduled release, your ads need a major refresh, and your dog has a stomach bug. Take a look at both your schedules and set realistic expectations for what can be written when. Crushing out half the book in the last two weeks and squeezing your editor for a ridiculous turnaround quickly flips what started life as a fun project into a stressful pain in the arse.

Assess for Professional Standing

Start out doing some research. Plug your potential collaborator's name into an online search. Check out their website for any information about their previous works or other creative partnerships. If they are affiliated with a company or organization, search those as well. You don't want to start down the road of a collaboration and find out later that your coauthor is in legal hot water or espouses a political position you find insupportable.

If your own search turns up no cause for alarm, tap into these great resources:

- **The Alliance of Independent Authors' Watchdog Desk** monitors the indie publishing industry as part of ALLi's Ethical Self-Publishing Campaign based on a Code of Standards for ethical authors and ethical services. https://www.allianceindependentauthors.org/watchdog/

- **Writer Beware** is a blog and email newsletter that provides news and commentary related to the all-too-wide world of literary scams and schemes. These posts are available to everyone, but Writer Beware will also respond to queries from individuals as their schedule permits. Matty has tapped into these resources to vet guests for *The Indy Author Podcast.* https://writerbeware.blog/

The reason for doing this research into a potential collaborator you don't know personally is obvious, but you should take these steps even if you do know them personally. There can be plenty going on in the lives of even our closest associates that we're not aware of. Don't allow yourself to be taken by surprise by bad news.

Assess Their Previous Work

If the potential collaborator has published previously, check out their work, especially if they have indie published. Is their cover of a professional quality? Does their content reflect professional editing? If their previous work includes nonfiction, is the material logically and thoughtfully presented? Is their style one that seems compatible (not necessarily identical) to your own? Never assume that a creator will treat a coauthored project with more care than a solo project.

Assess for Professional Experience

Are you and your potential coauthor at a similar point in your author careers? Have you published a similar number of books (even if that number is zero)? Discrepancy in the length of your résumés isn't necessarily a showstopper, but you need to factor it in.

For example, if an indie author and a traditionally published author plan to enter into a collaboration to indie publish a book, then the author with the indie experience might end up doing more of the work of loading the book to the distribution platforms or of coaching their coauthor through the process. If the authors plan to pursue a traditional deal for their book, then the trad published author might end up doing more of the legwork related to getting the manuscript in front of the agents and editors.

If your professional experience is similar, then you can divide up publishing tasks based on to other considerations, like time availability.

Carefully consider whether to work with an author who has never published anything, either indie or traditional. Do they have several manuscripts in their desk that have never come to fruition? If an author is unable to complete a project on their own, it's unlikely that their finishing energy will be ignited by a coauthored project. Don't get yourself in a position where you're having to coax (or strong-arm) work out of your coauthor … and don't put another writer in the position of having to do that for you.

Discussing a Potential Collaboration with the Coauthor

Once you've conducted your own assessment of your potential collaborator as described above, the rest of the considerations for assessing an opportunity will require conversation with that person.

Assess for Topic Knowledge

By this, we mean assessing your potential coauthor's knowledge about the topic of your book. You probably have some overlap in knowledge if a collaborative project is on the table, but an exact overlap of knowledge is not necessarily required or even desirable.

For example, when Mark Lefebvre and Matty coauthored *Taking the Short Tack*, they knew that Mark had far more experience with the traditional short fiction market than she did, so it was a foregone conclusion that he would need to provide the content for chapters related to that topic. Matty didn't necessarily have more information than Mark about indie publishing short fiction, but she did know enough that she could draft chapters related to that topic and then solicit additional information from Mark. They used the differences in their knowledge as a way of dividing up responsibility for drafting various chapters.

Similarly, when Michael and Matty coauthored *From Page to Platform*, Michael had more experience with paid speaking engagements, while Matty could speak to podcasting, acting as a panelist or panel moderator, and author readings, so we divided the drafting of chapters that way.

Of course, if the coauthored work will require research into a topic area neither of you is familiar with, you will need to factor in the time and effort needed to do that research.

Assess for Writing Skills

Coauthoring a book means that it's vital to understand your potential collaborator's writing skills. Ideally, they are on par with yours—or perhaps even better, giving you a chance to hone your craft.

But as Dr. Katherine Ramsland, coauthor of ten coauthored books and multiple articles, says, a significant discrepancy in writing skills risks ...

———————————————

... working with someone who writes in a substandard way, leaving you to repair it while they get paid. Avoid

this by learning a lot about your co-author's style and prior publications, if any, or interview others who have worked with the person to discover their habits.

Knowing that writing skills aren't your potential partner's strong suit doesn't necessarily have to scuttle the collaborative project; the other person may bring more topic knowledge or publishing know-how to the project, making it worth your time to spend more time editing their work. However, consider that this works best if your collaborator recognizes the need for more polishing of their words. If they believe their work is fine as is, are you willing to have the difficult conversation with them about your own, different perspective?

Assess for Publishing Skills

Consider the skills each of you brings to the collaboration in addition to subject matter expertise and writing skills. This might be an understanding of interior and exterior book design, book production and distribution, marketing and promotion best practices, or IP copyright knowledge. It might include skills not specific to writing and publishing. For example, Matty brings many years of project management experience to her collaborative projects; Michael brings business skills and knowledge from the corporate world.

As with knowledge of the topic of your collaboration, there are pros and cons to you and your collaborator having overlapping skills or complementary skills. Having overlapping skills enables you to serve as backup to the other on task assignments; having complementary skills means an easy way of dividing up tasks and may mean your skills cover a broader range of tasks.

Assess for Genre

Partnering with an author who writes and publishes in the

same genre as you do makes it more likely that you will be successful in bringing their fans into your camp and vice versa.

If you are thinking of collaborating with an author who is established in a different genre—for example, your background is in narrative nonfiction and their background is in instructional how-to books—then you need to consider how you will accommodate these different approaches. Will one of you flex into the other's genre, or will you try to meld them into a genre that combines aspects of both (which can be tricky from a marketing point of view)? How will you set the appropriate expectations for both your fan bases so that your followers aren't unpleasantly surprised if the co-written work differs markedly from "their" author's work?

Unsure what your coauthor's genre is? Ask them what they consider to be popular comparable titles, or comps, for their published work. (You can learn even more if you ask them what they think the popular comps will be for your coauthored work.)

Assess for Reader Goals

Similar to assessing for genre, you and your coauthor should also be on the same page about what you want readers to take away from the book. Do you want to educate them? Entertain them? Inspire them? What would you want your readers' next steps to be when they finish your book?

Start with the goal you have for your readers—the reader's desired transformation—and work your way backwards to the point where they stumble upon the product page and read the book description. You and your coauthor should agree on what you want this process to look like. (Understanding this process will also help you stay on track as you are writing.)

For example, if you and your coauthor are writing a book about nutrition, what does the reader's transformation look like? Working backward, the ultimate goal might be empowering readers to take control of their nutrition once and for all and living their best lives, full of energy and happiness fueled by healthy food. To get there, your book might focus on helping readers master simple, healthy cooking at home, showing them that eating well doesn't have to be expensive or time-consuming. You could structure the book around easy-to-follow recipes, tips for affordable grocery shopping, and quick meal planning strategies. If the book itself is short, practical, and approachable—just like the lifestyle you're promoting—you'll want your book description to reflect those qualities, emphasizing that readers will quickly and confidently start their journey to better health.

This is how you start at the transformation and reverse-engineer your way to the point of sale. You might not be able to provide such a fully fleshed-out document of your desired reader experience this early in the process, but starting this conversation early will help get you in alignment and might even identify opportunities that each of you individually might not have come up with.

Assess for Professional Goals

Ask your potential coauthor about their professional goals for the book and share your own. Ideally, those goals will match. If both of you are enthusiastic about using a book as a way of generating an additional stream of income, you will both be more likely to be willing to engage in ongoing promotion activities. If you both want to use a book as a calling card for speaking opportunities and are less concerned about sales outside those venues, then you might agree to invest less time in joint promotion activities after launch.

As with many of these considerations, a mismatch isn't necessarily a showstopper but should be factored in upfront. If Author A is looking for income and Author B is looking for a calling card for speaking engagements, then you might agree that you will share royalties 50/50 for some period of time after the launch, and then, on the assumption that Author A will be doing most of the promotional work, might adjust the royalty split to 75/25 after that date. (Make sure in advance that the distribution platforms you use support such a change, or that you have factored in the need to manage this manually.)

Assess for Personal Goals

It's difficult to separate professional goals from personal goals, and sometimes the true personal goals are masked even from the person who has them. This makes an assessment of personal goals difficult to conduct and even harder to negotiate.

A writer may want to enter into the collaboration simply to achieve a personal goal of seeing a book with their name on it on a virtual or actual bookshelf, but not necessarily have a personal goal of working on their craft or of engaging fully in the publishing work needed. And they may be unwilling to admit this to their potential coauthor and even to themselves.

Probing a coauthor's personal goals can be difficult, especially if you don't already have an established relationship, so in some cases you may need to look out for telltale signs or warnings about possible pitfalls. Does one of you try to steer the conversation exclusively to the money-making potential while the other one tries to steer it to the book as a résumé-builder? Does one talk about the many projects they are working on while the other talks about an event a few months away that would be a great venue for selling the book? This is not a matter of one person being right and one being wrong—although of course if you hear something that seems underhanded or downright illegal, that's a hard "no" for a collaboration—but rather of degree of alignment.

Assess for Personal Compatibility

We don't mean to suggest that you and your coauthor must have the same personality traits. In fact, different traits can be useful—for example, the more introverted partner in the collaboration might take on more of the behind-the-scenes tasks while the more extroverted partner takes on more promotional tasks.

But you are going to be working closely with this person on a creative endeavor, and you want to make sure that that experience is pleasant, or at least satisfying, for both of you. Of course, this is fairly easy to judge if you know the author personally, but you can get clues regarding compatibility in other ways.

Pay attention to what others in the writing and publishing communities say about them. Our collaborations have been with people who are respected, admired, and trusted by their fellow authors, and our experiences with them one-on-one bore out this assessment.

Check out their social media presence; you can learn a lot about a person by what they choose to share and how they interact with others online. Do they tend to be supportive? Confrontational? How would you feel about having them represent a jointly produced work in public forums?

If possible, watch videos of the author being interviewed or giving a presentation. Do they seem personable and respectful, or do they put themselves at odds with the audience? If they act unprofessionally when they know a camera or mic is on them, they are unlikely to be better one-on-one.

What kind of energy do they give off? There is nothing intrinsically right or wrong with being high energy or low key, but in a collaborative situation, the first might seem overbearing to their partner and the second might seem disengaged.

You don't need to be buddies with your coauthor, but you do need to respect them personally and professionally. As author Bruce Robert Coffin says, "There will be stressful times when things don't go well, and that trust and mutual respect will get you through it."

Test the Waters

If the opportunities offered for coauthoring sound appealing, consider testing the waters with a small project. For example, you might collaborate on an article or a presentation on the proposed topic with your potential coauthor. Or give yourselves an exploratory, no obligations "trial period" where you work together for a few weeks on a few chapters and see what it is like to collaborate. At the end of the trial period, if both of you don't agree to continue, then you can scrap the project and walk away.

Trust Your Gut

Entering into a collaborative project is a significant undertaking and you might find you have some butterflies in your stomach as time to fully commit to this collaboration draws near. (This is a creative marriage, and you're headed for the altar!) Some butterflies are to be expected, but you also need to trust your gut. Even if your potential coauthor seems to have passed all the checks described above, if you still don't feel good about the collaboration, don't ignore that feeling. Just say no.

If you need to say no to a potential collaboration, what's the best way to do that? Read on.

How to Say No

You may decide that a collaboration isn't a good fit. Perhaps their style doesn't mesh with yours or exploratory meetings suggest that you may be personally incompatible. And don't talk yourself into the idea that you can tough it out for the months or years you will be working with your coauthor; you will both own the copyright to any work you create for your lives plus 70 years, and there will be some level of interaction between you and your collaborator—or even between your heirs and theirs—for that time. If there is even a slight chance that this person may not be a good fit for you, we recommend severing the relationship at this point; the earlier you make this decision, the easier it will be.

How do you say no? Do it gently but decisively. Don't do it via email. Be honest and respectful, focusing on the fit rather than making it personal. You might say something like, "I've given this a lot of thought, and I don't think our working styles are as compatible as they would need to be for a successful collaboration," or "I really respect your work, but I'm realizing that this project isn't the right fit for me." Avoid long explanations or blaming either party. Keep the conversation positive, thank them for their time and interest, and wish them well. The goal is to end the conversation clearly and kindly, without leaving the door open to confusion or second-guessing.

Then, walk away. If you can remain friends, then do whatever you can to preserve the relationship. But if you are not a fit, do not collaborate. In the long term, you are doing both yourself and the other author a favor.

(We will address how to extract yourself from a collaboration once it has begun in the section "Extracting Yourself from an In-Process Collaboration.")

For Your Consideration

Consider the following and capture your responses in the downloadable document available at TheIndyAuthor.com/Collaborate. For this section …

What is your assessment of your potential collaborator related to the following considerations?

- Professional standing
- Previous work
- Professional experience
- Topic knowledge
- Writing skills
- Publishing skills
- Genre
- Reader goals
- Professional goals
- Personal goals
- Personal compatibility

ALIGNING ON EXPECTATIONS

You and another author have decided to pursue a collaboration —congratulations! The next step is to come to an agreement on the project. We recommend doing this in two steps:

- Aligning on Expectations
- Formalizing the Partnership

Aligning with your potential coauthor on expectations for the collaboration will ease the process of crafting a contract you will both be happy with but will also highlight if the collaboration shouldn't go further.

Matty polled past guests of *The Indy Author Podcast* about any coauthoring tips they had to share or pitfalls they could help writers avoid, and almost every response emphasizes the vital importance of coming to an agreement about the nature of the collaboration before entering into the project. Here's what author Kevin Tumlinson had to say:

> *Have a lot of long discussions up front about how this is going to work. Are you dividing duties? One person writes while the other edits? Does that person write the full draft, or do it chapter by chapter? How will you split royalties? How will you handle file sharing? Think of the most nightmare scenarios you can come up with and discuss those together at length before either of you so much as drafts an outline or puts words on the screen. Coauthoring gets a lot smoother and easier when everyone knows the rules and agrees to them up front. Prepare for the worst so you won't have to deal with the worst.*

Aligning on expectations upfront enables the formalization in a contract to be a simple acknowledgement of the agreements you've already come to. It also makes the decision to discontinue pursuing a collaboration less painful than if you've signed a contract and then discover unresolvable issues as you begin your collaborative work.

If you don't feel comfortable working with your potential coauthor to agree on and capture in writing the rules of your business relationship, you're not likely to feel comfortable working with them on your creative project; coming to an agreement that is formalized in a contract is a great final step to understanding if this relationship will be successful. As author Lee Savino says, "Don't sign a contract with anyone you wouldn't trust with a simple handshake agreement."

Pro Tip: As you capture your alignment on these items, also note why you made certain decisions. For example, if you decide not to produce a hardcopy edition of your book, note the reason (*the authors believe that the audience for a hardcopy* *edition is small enough not to merit the time and expense of producing that edition).* That can save you hours of uncertainty and speculation later when you and your collaborator wonder, "Why didn't we create a hardcover edition ...?"

Use this section to talk through the key areas of alignment with your prospective coauthor; we've provided a downloadable document, linked at the end of this section, for you to capture these agreements.

A final note before we dive in: throughout this section, you'll see a theme of deciding who has the final say for various decisions related to the work. As experienced coauthor Bruce Robert Coffin advises:

For anyone considering entering into a coauthoring contract, it is important at the start that everyone understands who has the final say whenever a creative disagreement crops up. In other words, someone has to be in charge. As long as both authors understand this going in, there will be far less turmoil during the project.

Unlike in the section on "Exploring the Opportunity," where we started with the most strategic consideration and became gradually more tactical, in this section on "Aligning on Expectations," we start with the tactical and lead to the strategic, since it's not possible to productively discuss royalty splits before understanding things like roles and responsibilities and project costs.

Content

We recommend that you and your collaborator write an "About This Book" or equivalent document as part of the process of aligning on expectations. Not only will it provide a valuable basis for your project, but it may also form a section of the book itself.

For example, in our early discussions about this book, we agreed that *Collaborate to Create* would:

- Focus on a collaborative project with two (not more) authors
- Exclude information on anthologies
- Exclude information on ghostwriting
- Focus specifically on nonfiction

We also documented our rationale for each of these decisions. For example, we captured our reasons for having *Collaborate to Create* focus on books with no more than two authors (because we believe that is a good way for authors to begin their venture into collaborative work and also because it avoided us having to deal with the stylistic awkwardness of *your coauthor or coauthors*). We captured our decision to focus specifically on nonfiction (because some early attempts at incorporating fiction forced an unwieldy structure).

Not only was this information vital for us as we began drafting the book, but we were also able to share it with you the reader in the "What We Cover" section of this book to ensure we and you are in alignment on what the book will address.

By talking through these considerations early, we avoided issues like one of us spending time researching and writing up information on a topic that the other assumed to be out of scope.

Other key factors related to contact to agree on are:

- Target audience (for example, *beginners in this topic area* or *experts in this topic area*)

- Bullet points of topics to be covered
- Rough estimate of word count of final work – This may change as you work on the project, but it helps if you start out with aligned expectations.
- High level positioning statement (for example, *the most comprehensive book available on this topic* or *an easy read that will give you the basics in a couple of hours*)
- Materials beyond the book (for example, a workbook)

Roles and Responsibilities

Documenting some high-level decisions about roles and responsibilities smooths the way for the collaboration. For example, Matty and Michael's coauthored books are published under Matty's William Kingsfield Publishers imprint, so she does most of the work related to getting the book uploaded to the various retail platforms. Michael has more experience with Amazon advertising that Matty does, so he takes responsibility for that work (although the costs for the ads are shared).

When author Todd Harra entered into a coauthoring agreement, he and his collaborator worked out a division of responsibility that made sense based on their areas of expertise and interest:

Our division of labor was pretty clear. He had the idea, he carried the burden of gathering the content, and I was responsible for writing it, pitching it, getting it sold, and then handling the editing. He took on the marketing. He was using the project to drum up business for his mortuary as well as to raise funds for a charity, so he had plenty of reasons to put a lot of effort into promoting the book.

It worked out really well because there wasn't any crossover. He wasn't interested in writing, and at that time, I wasn't interested in promotion. This clear division of labor made for a great partnership, and it even translated into a second book.

Understanding at a high level the division of labor for the content creation—and who has final say—is another great topic to align on upfront. Author Michael Bracken says:

Trying to be co-equals in every aspect of drafting a manuscript can lead to situations where it's impossible to make decisions when co-authors disagree. This can lead to rancor, which damages a working relationship, and/or to stasis, where projects cease to make progress. By agreeing in advance which of the writing partners will make final decisions and create the final draft, many potential problems are eliminated. The partner who is not making the final decisions can express their opinion but, if overruled, will accept decisions and move forward.

When collaborators work on multiple projects together, the final decision maker might not always be the same partner. If there's an imbalance in experience, perhaps the experienced partner always makes the final decisions. In cases where the collaborators have similar levels of experience, the decision maker might be the partner who brought the idea or the project to the team.

For *Collaborate to Create*, Matty as the publisher holds the tiebreaker vote when it comes to decision-making, a responsibility we formalized in our contract.

Project Management

Discuss at a high level who will be responsible for managing the project, and how that person will manage it, especially because people's level of comfort with the structure of a managed project can vary wildly. The good news is you and your coauthor don't need to have the same perspective on this—in fact, that can be detrimental if you're both unstructured—but you do both need to agree to conform to some form of project management to keep the project under control.

Matty and Michael's collaboration was a case of coauthors having similar skills in terms of project management and organization. This meant that if one of us proposed using a task management app or spreadsheet to track information related to the project, the other wasn't likely to balk.

On the other hand, Matty's collaboration with Mark Lefebvre was a case of coauthors having dissimilar skills or at least preferences. In a conversation in Episode 14 of *The Indy Author Podcast*, "Collaborating on *Taking the Short Tack*," Mark called it *the yin and yang of collaboration*.

It was an eye-opening exercise to see how somebody who's actually organized and does project management stuff completes a project. You brought discipline and organization to my world of writing that even in my former collaborations was never that organized.

—Mark Leslie Lefebvre, Episode 14 of *The Indy Author*

Podcast: "Collaborating on *Taking the Short Tack: Creating Income and Connecting with Readers Using Short Fiction*"

This doesn't mean that Mark is incapable of this type of organization; he has played the project manager role many times. But project manager is not Mark's favorite role, so he was happy for Matty to take on that responsibility for *Taking the Short Tack*. In turn, Matty appreciated Mark's accommodation of her preference for organization.

A collaborative project will be most effective if you tap into the special skills of each collaborator, and if you establish a relationship that will enable them to exercise those skills.

Project Costs

Discuss what types of costs will arise during the course of the project and in the years to follow, an estimate of what these costs might be, and how those costs will be covered. These might include costs related to:

- Editing / Proofreading
- Cover Design
- Advertising / Promotion
- ISBNs
- Copyright Registration

Will the collaborators split these costs equally? Will the partner under whose imprint the book will be published shoulder more of the cost?

Branding

Discuss what branding will be used for the book. For example, both *Taking the Short Tack*, which Matty coauthored with Mark Lefebvre, and *From Page to Platform*, which Matty and Michael coauthored, use Matty's The Indy Author branding (which makes sense, since the books are published under Matty's William Kingsfield Publishers imprint). In these cases, this mainly means that the cover and interior design match Matty's other nonfiction books.

Editing

- Will you engage a professional editor? Will you hire different editors for different edits (developmental, copyedit, proofread)?
- If you will hire a professional editor, how will the expense be covered? Who has final say in choosing the editor? Who has final say in how to act on the editor's input?
- If you will not hire a professional editor, how will these types of edits be performed?

Interior Formatting

- Will you engage a professional book formatter?
- If yes, how will the expense be covered (both for the initial formatting and any changes needed after initial publication)? Who has the final say in choosing the formatter? Who has final say about the format?
- If no, who will do the formatting? Which app will you use?

Cover Design

- Will you engage a professional cover designer?
- If yes, how will the expense be covered? Who will prepare the design brief? Who has final say in

choosing the designer? Who has final say about the design? Who will engage the designer?
- If no, who will do the cover design?

Production

- What formats (ebook, paperback, hardcover, large print, audio, etc.) will you produce?
- What platforms will you use to distribute each format?
- If producing audio, who will narrate it? How will the expense be covered?
- Who will be primarily responsible for coordinating the production?

Distribution

- On what platforms will you distribute each format of your book?
- Who will be primarily responsible for coordinating distribution?

Marketing

- Will there be an online presence (for example, website or page) for the book and, if yes, who will manage this?
- Will you promote the book on social media? If yes, who will be responsible for creating content, and who will be responsible for posting it on the various platforms?
- How will you split the marketing budget?

Promotion

This early in the process, it's difficult to have a clear idea of the promotions you might want to run for your book, but at a minimum, discuss:

- Who needs to approve price changes for promotions, and who will execute these in the backend systems?
- Where will you promote the book?

Schedules and Deadlines

This early in the process, it's difficult to pin down schedules and deadlines with any level of precision, so focus on general timeframes (for example, targets by month) and discuss what types of situations might require you to reconsider those timeframes.

The longer you anticipate the project will last, the more flexible you will need to be about schedules and deadlines. It's impossible to anticipate what issues might arise during a collaborative project. While we were working on *From Page to Platform*, a pipe burst in Matty's second floor master bathroom, flooding part of the second floor, the first floor, and the basement, and sending her writing and publishing plans into disarray as she and her husband dealt with the aftermath. Michael has needed to delay projects due to illness and injury.

The key is to maintain flexibility. If you're aligned on the general trajectory of the project, then navigating these types of situations is easier.

Administrative / Legal

Talk through the administrative side of publishing, including the following.

Under whose accounts will the book be set up (for example,

on retail or aggregator platforms)? This will probably be the same as the imprint it's published under. Unless you and your coauthor are planning to build an entire business around your book (consulting, speaking engagements, etc.)—don't set up a separate account or imprint for a coauthored book.

What happens if one author dies or becomes incapacitated? In our coauthoring agreements, we list our spouses as our beneficiaries and alternate contacts. Include a provision that allows the surviving author to take control of the book on the retail, production, and distribution platforms so that they can switch the books to their own account. (If you'd like more information on estate planning for authors, check out Michael's book *The Author Estate Handbook*.)

Royalties

Discuss what percentage of royalties will go to each author. (This is an area you will probably want to think through yourself before broaching the topic with your potential partner.)

In general, we recommend a 50/50 split. In fact, a 50/50 split is a good way of setting the expectation of an equal division of responsibility. If one collaborator requests an unequal division that favors themselves, they not only imply that they will be doing more of the work but also risk creating tension or resentment from the outset.

Of course, there might be valid reasons for considering a split other than 50/50. Perhaps you are an author earlier in your career and are approaching a well-known author with an enormous fan base to propose a coauthored project. The benefits you expect to gain from that author's celebrity might make it worthwhile for you to accept a lower—perhaps significantly lower—royalty percentage. Or you might find yourself in a situation where your potential partner is happy to provide content for the book but doesn't want to get involved in the production, distribution, marketing, or promotion work, which might merit you receiving a higher royalty percentage.

If you find there is a reason for one author to receive a higher royalty percentage than the other, don't quibble over a percentage point; round to the nearest 5 or 10 (for example, 60/40 or 75/25).

Also discuss the mechanism for dividing royalties. Ensuring that the distribution of royalties is automated is a priority. Consider that you will be earning royalties from your collaboration for years, if not decades, after publication. Manually calculating and distributing royalties may seem manageable for a few months, but do you really want to be doing it a year after publication? Five years? Ten years? Do you want to require your heirs to be handling this task?

Matty and Michael chose to distribute *From Page to Platform* to most retail platforms via Draft2Digital because of its automated royalty-splitting functionality. We were willing to give up a percentage of royalties from platforms to which we would normally distribute direct in exchange for the long-term benefits this automation would provide. (In addition, using as few distributors or aggregators as possible also means it's far easier to run reports and to track down answers to any questions related to royalties.)

IP and Rights

Note that **copyright ownership does not equal royalty split percentage**. Both you and your coauthor own the copyright equally. However, the split of the proceeds you receive from the royalties does not have to be equal, and it can also be different for each right you exploit. This is why it is crucial to discuss this upfront so there are no misunderstandings or hurt feelings when an opportunity presents itself.

Discuss the process by which you will assess opportunities to license your IP beyond your book—for example, for translations, online courses, and merchandise—should these opportunities arise. What criteria will you use for your assessment and what will the process be? If you can foresee the most likely licensing scenarios, discuss details like responsibility for pursuing opportunities and royalty splits.

Michael once worked on a collaboration where the coauthor had connections in the movie world. The coauthor wrote a screenplay based on the coauthored book and shopped it around Hollywood with the understanding that if they received an option, the coauthor would take a higher percentage of the proceeds because he did more work. When it comes to rights licensing, sometimes one partner plays a more active role than the other, and this should be considered upfront and reflected in the contract.

If the collaboration has the possibility of moving beyond one book, then consider what will happen if one collaborator loses interest but the other wants to carry the project forward. Todd Harra and his coauthor factored this into their alignment discussions and into their contract:

My coauthor couldn't go out and continue the franchise without my permission. If I decided, "You know what, go ahead, have at it. I'm just too tired, and I don't care if you do it," that would be my choice. But ultimately, it's my right to make that call.

Since then, I've done projects without him, but none of them have anything to do with the franchise we built together. Early on, we anticipated the possibility of success and asked ourselves, "If this takes off, how's it going to look for future projects?"

That's why it's so important to figure these things out

before you start. You need to put it down on paper: "How is this going to work moving forward?"

Use of AI

No discussion of writing and publishing work would be complete without some consideration of the role of artificial intelligence. AI has the potential to impact every aspect of our business and creative lives in ways we can't predict and perhaps can't even imagine, from brainstorming book titles or topics to drafting content to creating cover or interior images to creating marketing and promotion materials.

Early in the process, it's imperative to have a high-level agreement about the use—or non-use—of AI, recognizing that more detailed agreements may need to be negotiated as the project progresses. After all, an AI function that was unimaginable at the beginning of your project might be generally available later in your collaborative process.

We recommend that unless you are both committed to no use of AI in your collaborative work, you divide the discussion into its use for creating content and its use for supporting the publication and promotion of the work; people who would refuse to use AI for writing the book itself might be more comfortable using it to brainstorm ideas for topic areas to cover or to suggest text for social media posts.

In addition to moral considerations related to the use of AI, also factor in the legal considerations. AI is an ever-evolving field, and what is in vogue today will be obsolete tomorrow. Courts are also still weighing the impact of AI in our society and how it will shape our legal destiny.

In any case, make sure you and your coauthor agree at least at a high level about if and how AI will be used in your project. AI offers the ability to work more productively and collabora-

MATTY DALRYMPLE & M.L. RONN

tively in ways that we previously only dreamed of, but it also introduces some risk, so weigh your options carefully.

Additional Information

Collect any additional information that will be useful to your collaboration, including:

- Contact information (email address, physical address, phone number) for each author
- Alternate contact and their contact information
- Production specs (for example, fonts used for the interior and cover, brand colors, etc.)
- File locations if on shared platforms such as Google Drive or iCloud (more on that in the section "Choosing the Writing Platform")

For Your Consideration

Consider the following and capture your responses in the downloadable document available at TheIndyAuthor.com/Collaborate. For this section …

Capture the agreement between you and your collaborator regarding:

- Content
- Roles and responsibilities
- Project management
- Project costs
- Branding
- Editing
- Interior formatting
- Cover design
- Projection
- Distribution

- Marketing
- Promotion
- Schedules and deadlines
- Administrative / legal
- Royalties
- Use of AI

(You might want to capture this is a separate document that you can share with your collaborator.)

FORMALIZING THE PARTNERSHIP

If you've confirmed your alignment on the items above with your collaborator (and any other impacted parties, such as publishing houses or agents), you may be thinking, "We have everything we need right here! Why do I need to formalize our agreement in a contract?"

You don't enter into a contract because you distrust the other person. You enter into a contract to prove that you do trust them.

Another circumstance in which a contract is valuable is if it needs to speak for a person who is no longer available to speak for themselves; for example, the contracts we have for our coauthored books include provisions for what happens to the IP rights if one of us dies.

Contracts don't have to be long or complicated. The template contract that the Alliance of Independent Authors provides for its members is four pages long. The contracts Matty and Michael created for our coauthored books are about six pages each.

You don't have to start from scratch. Search online for *template for coauthoring contract* and scan the results for reputable names; a .org domain name will indicate that the provider of the template is a non-profit and is therefore not going to try to sell you products or services. Search for *SFWA model collaboration agreement* to check out the coauthoring contract template provided by the Science Fiction and Fantasy Writers Association (SFWA).

Of course, getting a legal professional involved provides another level of protection for both parties, as in the case of Todd Harra and his coauthor.

One of the most important things we did was hire an attorney to help us draft a contract. The contract outlined exactly what everyone's responsibilities would be, and the attorney went through every detail. It addressed scenarios like, "What happens if one of us dies?" or "What if the project doesn't get sold?" It even included a clause allowing the project to be bought back. Essentially, we considered every possible situation that could arise in this kind of business relationship. We split the attorney's fee 50/50. It wasn't a huge expense, but it gave us peace of mind. If something went sideways, we had a remedy in place instead of relying on a handshake agreement.

As Todd's comment reflects, it's important to remember that a contract protects not just you but your heirs, who could benefit from royalties and IP rights after your death. Make sure the person who will take over responsibility for your work should you die or become incapacitated understands the provisions of the contract.

Todd goes on to say:

At the time, I knew my coauthor. We'd met face-to-face and were, for all intents and purposes, friends. But anything can happen in business. Even if coauthors don't involve an attorney, they should at least sit down, write out an agreement that outlines the division of duties, and sign it.

This is especially critical if things don't go as planned or if there's a dispute. Who gets the manuscript? Who owns the intellectual property? Having something in writing ensures there's a clear path forward, even in challenging situations.

Finally, remember that signing a contract doesn't mean you are restricted by it as long as both parties agree to any changes. For example, after the publication of *Taking the Short Tack*, Mark Lefebvre and Matty signed an addendum to confirm the decision that the book would not be explicitly branded as part of The Indy Author series or incorporate The Indy Author logo, to formalize changes to the royalty-splitting process, and to confirm that each author would keep all royalties from their direct sales stores or in-person events. After the publication of *From Page to Platform*, Matty and Michael signed an addendum that covered how we would handle division of royalties from bundles each of us might create that included that book.

For Your Consideration

For this section, compare your "For Your Consideration" notes captured so far against your proposed contract to make sure all the appropriate items are covered.

MANAGING THE LOGISTICS

You've aligned on expectations and formalized your partnership in a contract; now it's time to plunge into the project!

Choosing the Writing Platform

The first decision you'll want to make is what platform or application you'll use for the actual writing of the book; this can be one of the most technically challenging parts of a coauthored project.

At the time of this writing, there is no bulletproof option that accommodates all the desired qualities of a coauthoring application: support for real-time collaboration within a shared document, the ability to log comments and track changes, version control, reliable backup functions, and robust formatting options, all within an attractive user interface.

We've listed below some of the platforms that we experimented with in our collaborations and have noted the pros and cons of each. You and your collaborator can weigh what features and functions are most and least important to you to make the best choice for your project.

Author-specific Writing Apps

Our survey of author-specific writing apps such as Scrivener didn't uncover any that we felt were good candidates for coauthoring for reasons including lukewarm user reviews regarding the coauthoring experience, a steep learning curve, and limited collaboration functions in comparison to the options listed below.

Google Docs

Pros:

- It's free and ubiquitous.
- It enables multiple users to edit the same document simultaneously. This can be especially valuable early in the process when you and your coauthor are capturing ideas for content and roughing out first drafts. For example, if you both have ideas for content to include in a chapter on a particular topic, you can just pop into the Google Doc and add that information with no further coordination needed.
- Revealing the sidebar provides a nice at-a-glance view of chapters and sections.
- Google stores a version history for reference.

Cons:

- Formatting options are limited.
- Using the mode "Suggesting" rather than "Editing" mimics an MS Word track changes-type function, but it's more awkward to use.
- Although it's difficult to point to a particular reason for this, we never found the Google Docs user interface to be conducive to creative work.

MS Word or Apple Pages

Pros:

- Almost everyone has one or the other of these programs (or free equivalents such as LibreOffice).
- The Tracked Changes function is easy to use. We strongly recommend implementing a schedule with your coauthor for regularly reviewing changes and either accepting them or flagging them for discussion. Letting changes build up for too long can result in a real review headache.
- In Microsoft Word, turning on View > Sidebar > Navigation provides an outline view of the book, which is invaluable for organizing the content.
- Apple Pages allows you to insert voice comments, which can be a great way to communicate complex thoughts about a topic to your collaborator.
- If you plan to format the book in Vellum, then Word (or a Pages export to Word) is the format you'll need for the Vellum import.

Cons:

- Because these are general apps and not specific to authors, they lack some desirable features like research or thorough outlining support.
- Although Microsoft claims that Word files stored on OneDrive can be simultaneously edited by multiple users, we didn't have much luck with this.
- Versioning and backup are more manual than with cloud-based docs. Once we reached a point where Google Docs was too cumbersome for our purposes and we made the decision to move to Word,

> Michael implemented an automated drive backup so that if we accidentally stepped on each other's edits, we could go back to an earlier version to retrieve any lost material.

Establishing a "Positive Exchange of Control"

One of the most important aspects of managing the manuscript of your coauthored work is to ensure that the "ownership" of the document is crystal clear at every step of the process. If you work on the document in a shared environment throughout the process, this is less of an issue, but it is vital if you are passing a document back and forth. Imagine a scenario where you and your coauthor both think you "own" the manuscript and are both making changes to separate copies; imagine the time, effort, and energy it would take to recombine those now separate documents back into one. It boggles the mind.

To avoid this situation, establish a "positive exchange of control." This is a concept Matty learned about when she was taking flying lessons. If the instructor handled the takeoff but then wanted the student to take over, the instructor would say "You have the flight controls," and the student would acknowledge the exchange by responding, "I have the flight controls." Then, just to be absolutely sure that everyone was in agreement about who was flying the plane, the instructor would again say, "You have the flight controls."

We got in the habit of using the phrase "you have the controls" when we passed ownership of the manuscript back and forth. You can further formalize this exchange by having the document in a different folder on your shared platform depending on who owns it; for example, Matty could move the manuscript from a "Matty" folder to a "Michael" folder when she was passing ownership to him.

You can ensure "positive exchange of control" and have a useful version history by creating a dedicated email thread to use for this purpose. Call it something that will distinguish it from any other emails you might exchange with your coauthor about your book: for example "You Have the Plane."

Early in the process, you and your coauthor might be passing control of the manuscript back and forth quite frequently, but you'll likely reach a point when one of you has the manuscript for days, weeks, or even months. Plan a periodic check-in on the ownership status, just to make sure everyone's in sync. For example, if you've passed the manuscript to your partner and expect they will have it for several weeks, check in after several weeks just to ensure that everything is on track. This avoids a situation not only where they might be stuck on something and are hesitant to ask for help, but also where each of you thinks the other holds "ownership."

We learned the benefit of this when Michael sent Matty an email letting her know that he was passing control of the manuscript back to her, but the email never went through. Michael assumed Matty was now working on the manuscript, and Matty assumed Michael was still working on it. Several weeks went by before we realized what had happened, and those were several weeks when no progress was being made on the work. When in doubt, check in.

Establishing Version Control

Agreeing on a naming convention for the manuscript files is helpful. When we reached the point in our project where we were passing one master file back and forth, we appended the word *MASTER* to the file name of the master version. When one of us then passed that file to the other one, the one doing the passing would make a copy with *AS OF YYYY MM DD* (indicating the year, month, and day of the versioned copy) appended to the file name. This also provided snapshots along the way in case, for example, we wanted to resurrect some content we had previously deleted. It also provided yet another form of data backup.

Choosing the Content Platforms

Once you have determined what platform or app you will use to write your book, you should also consider where you will host other content related to your book such as an outline, a project calendar, and marketing materials.

There are many file hosting choices, and as with writing apps, the landscape is always changing. However, here are a few of the tried-and-true platforms that are frequently used for their ease of use and reliability:

- Google Drive
- Dropbox
- Microsoft OneDrive
- iCloud

Your approach to assembling the content of your book may inform your choice of content platform. For example, if you use Google Docs, as we did, then Google Drive makes the most sense. If you use Apple Pages, iCloud would be a good choice.

If possible, pick one location and stick with it. During the creation of our first coauthored book, we were experimenting with different platforms, and our work got spread over several shared drives, which was inefficient and tedious to remediate.

Managing the Tasks

Your collaborative process will run much more smoothly if you have a centralized location for managing the tasks related to your project. We experimented with a task management-specific tool, and the functionality was handy (for example, providing the option of getting notifications of changes to tasks). However, we eventually moved to managing tasks in a Google Sheet on our shared drive to take advantage of the benefits of having most of the data and documents related to our project in one place.

We put together a simple spreadsheet to capture and track the following:

- Task
- Status (Pending, In Process, or Closed)
- Person responsible
- Target completion date
- Category (for example, Drafting, Editing, Distribution, Promotion, etc.)
- Notes

You can mimic some of the more specialized features of task management-specific tools within Google Sheets; for example, generating a notification by flagging your coauthor's name in a comment or assigning them follow-up via a note. This is a far better option than relying on collaborators to regularly check in on a task list; that approach might seem realistic early in the project, but you don't want to have to remember to do this throughout the life of the project (which, remember, will continue beyond the publication of the book).

A comprehensive task list not only addresses the tactical need to manage this work but can also serve as a valuable way of tracking the division of work across the entire project. At some point in the project, you're inevitably going to feel as if one or the other of the collaborators is taking on the lion's share of the work. But each contributor's amount of work will wax and wane depending on the stage of the project, each author's area of expertise, each author's available time, and so on. At any point in time, you may feel either that you're doing it all or that you're not pulling your weight; the key is whether the work is divided equitably across the whole of the project, and the task list will give you a macro view of the work.

Make sure you retain closed tasks in the list, since this will be necessary for the macro view. It will also enable you to have the full list of tasks available when you've completed the project, giving you the opportunity to review the work you did and refine it for future collaborative projects.

Choosing the Communications Platform

It's a good idea to agree on the primary platform you'll use for your communication—probably some combination of email or text—and which you will use in what circumstances. You might use text to ping your collaborator with a quick question but use email if the question is more complicated, not time critical, or requires some back-and-forth to come to a resolution.

However, we advise against using email or text as a project management tool. One issue is that it's unstructured. An email titled "Identifying Beta Readers" might wander into the topic of responsibility for coordinating with the proofreader and then into a question related to style guide elements. A more signifi-cant issue is that it doesn't provide an authoritative repository of decisions—would you think to look at the email titled "Identi-fying Beta Readers" for the answer to a question related to style guide elements? Most significantly, email doesn't enable an overall view of the project—for example, what are all the open issues that must be resolved before publication?

Instead, use email as a way of pointing your collaborator to the shared platform on which you are maintaining information on the topic. For example, rather than asking for a status on a task via email or text, send them a link to your shared task management document and ask them to post an update.

Backing Up Your Content

Michael likes to joke that he has an advanced degree in losing manuscripts. Things happen, especially in an age where everything is digital. Computers die, hard drives fail, programs don't save when you think they're saving. Coauthored manuscripts pose a higher risk of data loss because both authors may be working on a file at the same time. Or, if they're trading a file back and forth, the wrong version could be traded without either author realizing it.

Don't risk losing words or even your entire manuscript; have a backup plan in place. First, even though apps like Microsoft OneDrive and iCloud Drive offer autosave functions, don't rely on them because they can fail. Always assume that they will. And second, one author should take the lead in backing up the manuscript regularly to an external hard drive or use a hard drive backup service to ensure that backups of the manuscript exist. Agree on the frequency of backups. Early in the project, you might want to backup daily; later, when changes to the manuscript are less extensive, weekly might be sufficient.

For Your Consideration

Consider the following and capture your responses in the downloadable document available at TheIndyAuthor.com/Collabo rate. For this section …

Capture the agreement between you and your collaborator regarding your chosen:

- Writing platform
- "Positive exchange of control" process
- Version control
- Content platform
- Task management tool
- Communications platform
- Document backup plan

ASSEMBLING AND MANAGING THE TEAM

Of course, you and your collaborator constitute a team; but this section addresses management of others you may engage in your project, such as an editor or cover designer.

You will already have broached the topic of how extensive a team you planned to engage when you aligned on expectations. You also may have assigned responsibility for managing this team. Although different coauthors might take responsibility for coordinating with different team members—for example, one might coordinate with the editor and the other might coordinate with the cover designer—each person on your team should have one primary contact.

For example, you and your coauthor should discuss any issues related to cover design between yourselves, and then one of you should have responsibility for representing your agreed-upon instructions to the designer. Asking the designer to coordinate between you and your coauthor will create frustration on all sides, may end up costing you more money since this coordination with require more time from the designer, and will undermine your relationship with this member of your team.

For Your Consideration

Consider the following and capture your responses in the down-loadable document available at TheIndyAuthor.com/Collaborate. For this section …

Confirm the agreement between you and your collaborator regarding who will be the primary contact for each member of your team (for example, editor or cover designer).

DEFINING THE STANDARDS

Style Guide

Another step you can take to smooth the collaboration process is to agree on what resources you will use as style and editing guides. For example, since different automated spelling or grammar checkers—for example, the built-in functionalities in MS Word and ProWritingAid—sometimes make suggestions that contradict each other, agree on which you will use. You might also agree on what dictionary you will use when needed as a tiebreaker—for example, merriam-webster.com.

The *Chicago Manual of Style* (CMOS), commonly recommended for nonfiction, offers suggestions on how to handle the miscellaneous issues that pop up throughout a manuscript, such as date formatting and the capitalization of certain words such as French fries and bananas foster.

Some style and editing decisions will depend on the specifics of your project:

- Inclusion or avoidance of bulleted or numbered lists

(which can sometimes cause issues in the final
formatting for ebook and print)
- Use of *e.g. / i.e.* (which can sound strange in audio)
or *for example / in other words*
- Use or avoidance of phrases like *turn the page*
(which sounds out of place in audio)

Capture agreement on these in your shared document
library.

Drafting Conventions

Matty has developed a set of drafting "flags" for her solo work,
and Michael agreed to use them for our coauthored work. You
might find these useful as well!

- [Square brackets enclosing text] indicate questions
that need to be answered. Flagging open questions
in this way enables a search on "[" in the final edit to
ensure that all the questions have been answered.
- X followed by initials indicates a question for a
particular person. For example [*XMD Please rereview this section*] means that Matty should
rereview the section. This enables each author to
look for X and their own initials to find open
questions directed specifically at them.
- <Angle brackets> indicates words or phrases that
the author is <not totally happy with> and wants to
be sure to reassess during the drafting process. For
example, Matty wasn't thrilled with *not totally
happy with*, but she didn't want to slow her initial
drafting progress by spending time coming up with
something better in the moment. Be explicit with

your coauthor about whether you want them to take a crack at a better word or leave that to you.

Also, find a way to accommodate authorial oddities. (Nothing highlights the oddities of one's writing process faster than coauthoring.) For example, Matty tends to brainstorm solutions to problems on the page:

[*Should we target the book at published authors or writers at any stage of their careers? The benefit of specifying published authors is X. The benefit of casting the net wider, to include writers in general, is Y.*]

If Matty's coauthor encounters this note, what are they supposed to do with it? Weigh in on pros and cons of each option? Ignore it? There's no right or wrong answer, but you and your coauthor should be clear about the expectations upfront.

For Your Consideration

Consider the following and capture your responses in the downloadable document available at TheIndyAuthor.com/Collaborate. For this section ...

Confirm the agreement between you and your collaborator regarding:

- The resources you will use as your style guide(s)
- Any drafting conventions you will use in your coauthored work

CREATING THE CONTENT

No matter how detailed a scope document you and your collaborator have aligned on, the real test will come when you actually begin writing. In this section, we share the approach we have refined over two coauthored works for creating the content.

Negotiating the Plotter-to-Pantser Spectrum

It might seem on the surface as if the most challenging part of negotiating the actual writing process is if you and your collaborator are on opposite ends of the plotter-to-pantser spectrum. The plotter might want to have everything organized and outlined in advance. The pantser might want to just start writing and see where the process takes them. But the reality of co-creation means that neither extreme will work.

It's impossible to know where the interests, knowledge, and skills of your collaborator—and the fuel they might provide to your own inspiration—might take the project, and so trying to construct a full outline in advance doesn't take full advantage of the creative discoveries that collaboration can enable.

On the other hand, setting both collaborators off on a voyage of discovery writing is far too likely to result in each of you wandering off in incompatible directions, and so using a straight pantser approach is also fraught with peril.

Both collaborators need to be willing to walk a path midway between the extremes to gain the greatest creative benefits from coauthorship.

While Matty, with her love of the nautical metaphor for the writing craft, generally gravitates to the idea of framing out a boat—starting with a foundational "keel," adding the "ribs" of an outline, and proceeding to the "brightwork" of the final polish edit—a better metaphor for the coauthoring process might be creating a sculpture. This involves conceptualizing the final work, providing a frame for your creation, gathering the raw materials for construction, roughing out the shape, then modeling and refining.

Conceptualizing

As part of your process of "Aligning on Expectations," you and your coauthor will have agreed conceptually to the general scope of your work. Using our sculpture metaphor, you will have agreed on the subject of your sculpture—perhaps a stylized portrayal of two people shaking hands.

For *Collaborate to Create*, we had to agree on things like whether to cover both nonfiction and fiction, whether to make the material comprehensive or high-level, and whether to target beginning or experienced writers. (We decided to cover nonfiction only, make the material comprehensive, and target writers of any level of experience but who were planning for their first collaboration or wanting to improve the experience of a previous one.)

Creating the Framework

Based on that concept, we needed to create the framework of our book. In our metaphor, this would be the armature or supportive framework that provides stability to the sculpture. This framework further solidifies the scope of the work—for example, how much of the rest of the bodies of our hand-shaking subjects will be represented in the sculpture?

For a book, this involves creating an outline or table of contents.

AI can be applied to good effect in the framing stage if you and your coauthor have agreed to its use. Early in the process of planning for *Collaborate to Create*, we asked AI *what topics should be covered in a book about coauthoring nonfiction.* Many of the results confirmed topics we had already planned to cover; in a few cases, they identified additional topics we realized would be beneficial; in some cases, the suggestions weren't appropriate for what we wanted to accomplish but prompted us to refine our scope statement for the book.

Gathering the Raw Material

Once you have a frame in place, you'll have a better idea of the type of material you will need to flesh it out. In our sculpture metaphor, we equate this to digging the clay out of the ground, and both authors can have a hand in this.

Probably the easiest approach for gathering materials is in the case where you and your coauthor each have a different area of expertise, and once you have agreed on the book's **concept** and created the **framework**, you can, for a time at least, work on your portions of the book independently. For example, for our first coauthored book, *From Page to Platform*, we agreed that Matty would draft the sections on author readings and panels, and that Michael would draft the sections on "the author on the road."

For sections where both collaborators have expertise, you can gather raw materials via virtual meetings or exchanges of emails and texts. Another great way to collect content is for you and your coauthor to interview each other about the topic of the book. This can not only generate fodder for the book, but video excerpts of your conversations can serve as great promotional material!

In some cases, it may be easier for one author to take the lead in creating a first draft either for a chapter or the entire manuscript, with the other author following with editing. There is no right or wrong way—just the way that works for you.

Roughing Out

As you collect the raw material for your book, you will need to arrange it logically within the book's frame.

After our experiments during the creation of *From Page to Platform*, we decided for *Collaborate to Create* that it would be beneficial to assign one person—Matty—as the "arranger" of the information. Matty assembled the material in Word, knowing from our work on our first book that Word would work best for us, especially since our process assumed only one of us would be working on the file at any one time.

In some cases, the assembly meant just slotting content into the agreed-upon outline. In other cases, the process of assembly identified opportunities for new content. If a section needed more content and the topic lay in Michael's area of expertise—for example, estate planning for authors—Matty could ask Michael to send content related to that topic.

The advantage of having one person assemble the material is that it avoids the inefficiencies of both authors possibly working on similar material, unaware of what the other is doing. It enables one person to retain an overall sense of the project, so that they can issue an alert if, for example, some content feels out-of-scope, or one topic is generating loads of content while another is as yet unaddressed.

Often, it is during this roughing out stage that the themes of the book will become clearer. For example, for *Taking the Short Tack*, this was when it became clear that the book's two focuses would be creating income and connecting with readers (which became the subtitle).

Modeling

The modeling stage of creating a sculpture involves shaping and texturizing. In our coauthored work, in means refining the roughed-out work.

Until this point in the process, the person responsible for assembling the raw materials has held the master version of the manuscript. But before you enter into the next stage—refining— it's important for both authors to review the work in its rough form and buy into the direction the work is taking before you proceed.

One of the most mentally challenging parts of collaboration is being willing to share unpolished material with your collaborator. We authors sometimes struggle with being willing to accept that a rough draft can be rough, even when we are the only ones who will see it. How much more difficult it is to share that rough draft with someone else!

But this is an intrinsic part of coauthoring. You don't want to polish a chapter and then share it with your coauthor only to find out that, due to a miscommunication, they have written a nearly identical chapter, or that you've expressed a position or a recommendation they can't support. Far better to make these discoveries in a rough draft when course-correction is easier.

To facilitate this stage, we developed a system for logging and tracking questions and comments. If Matty had a question or comment for Michael, she would enter the question in square brackets and begin the comment with *XML*. For example:

[*XML Do you think this would make more sense in the next section?*]

Michael would prepend his questions and comments for Matty with *XMD*.

The benefit of this was that each of us could search for square brackets to find any questions or comments remaining in the manuscript and could search for *X* plus our initials to find those we specifically needed to address.

As with much else about coauthoring, the keys to navigating this stage successfully are alignment and communications. Be clear what expectation each of you should have of the other's roughed-out work—for example, that this is not the time for detailed copy- and line-editing. At this stage, you're looking for input about whether each of you is headed in the direction the other expected and whether the content is generally something you agree with.

You're bound to run into differences of opinion on what should be included. You'll have to "choose your hill to die on," knowing that you can't die on every hill, and neither can your coauthor. Ultimately, impasses like this will be negotiations. This is a normal part of the creative process. As author Kevin Tumlinson says:

At some point, the two of you are going to disagree on how the book should go forward—headbutting is bound to happen when you have two creatives working on the same project. Maybe one of you wants to include a chapter on taxes and the other thinks it's a complete bore. You might try compromise. Maybe you don't want the chapter on taxes, but if your partner will let you include your chapter on juggling, you can live with it. If compromise doesn't work, agree on how to resolve those issues ahead of time. Maybe you have a mediator—a neutral third party who gets to make the binding decision. Maybe you agree to a coin flip. As long as you both know in advance what it is, and both commit to it being the deciding factor, you'll breeze through.

The alignment work you and your coauthor did upfront will serve you well throughout this process.

Refining

To continue our sculpture metaphor, once you and your collaborator are in agreement on the general "model" of your work, a process that may stretch over several iterations, the next step is the refining process—smoothing out surfaces and forms.

We recommend that each author make a final refinement pass through the document with Track Changes or equivalent turned on. (At this point, only one author is working in the master manuscript file at a time, so one author will complete this pass and then pass it to the other author for their input using your agreed-upon "positive exchange of control" process.)

Whereas in the roughing out and modeling stages, you might have been posting your input as a question (for example, *Should we recommend approach A or approach B?*), at this point it's probably better just to make your desired changes, clearly marked with Track Changes so the coauthor can appeal if they don't agree.

Some of the changes made in this pass with be straight editorial corrections and will be facilitated if you have established some standards upfront (see the section on "Defining the Standards").

Some of the issues will be nitpicks; for example, you might use a pet phrase that irritates your coauthor. Some aspects may be more stylistic—for example, ensuring a consistent tone or voice throughout. (This assumes that consistent tone is something you have defined as a goal versus, for example, a coauthored book where one author is "posing" as a naïve questioner and the author is "posing" as the expert answerer, in which case consistency of tone is not necessarily needed.)

We knew that our coauthored work would benefit from a consistent style, but our styles for our individual works are quite different: Matty has a more formal style while Michael has a more casual style. As the designated publisher, Matty had the final say in the stylistic decisions, but she worked to retain the friendly, approachable tone that makes Michael's writing so engaging, and kept an eye out for opportunities to make her own contributions a bit less formal. Michael remained cognizant of his tone and that it didn't go too casual in order to blend better with Matty's voice. The result was that we met each other in a special common ground that became our unified coauthor voice.

If a consistent style is desired, one person should have the final say. As author Michael Bracken says, "Having one partner responsible for the final draft ensures that the finished manuscript has a single voice."

Pave the way to a smooth refinement process by being explicit with your coauthor about how you want to receive their input—via email or in a virtual meeting? As they find it or consolidated? See the section "Negotiating the Process" for more specifics.

Keeping It Clean

If you use a change tracking function so that you and your coauthor can see the changes the other has made, the manuscript can get messy looking if you display the changes. However, if you hide the changes, you may not fully factor in a change your coauthor has made—for example, they may have deleted a section but you, not realizing it has been deleted, continue referencing it in the material you're writing.

We've found the best way to avoid this is for each author to frequently review the changes the other person has made and either accept them or add a note directly in the manuscript explaining any concerns or reservations. This means you can enjoy the benefits of displaying the pending changes, but the manuscript isn't full of distracting red text, strikethroughs, and comments in the margins.

But keep in mind that you have to trust your coauthor enough that at some point, perhaps late in the editing process, you can discontinue mutual review of every change; if you continue to require that throughout the entire process, you'll never reach the end.

Once you and your coauthor are happy with the refinements you've made, it's time to solicit input from others.

SOLICITING INPUT

Soliciting input from others is a vital part of creating a professional-level book, and we'll review the three primary types of input you'll solicit—from beta readers, from an editor, and from a proofreader—in this section.

Engaging Beta Readers

Beta readers provide feedback on a manuscript from a typical reader's perspective. They serve as an impartial third party who can provide invaluable input on everything from stylistic aspects to substantive content issues. Matty reports that it took her audiobook narrator—a sort of "beta listener"—to point out that she tends to overuse the word "evidently" in her novels.

A benefit of co-writing is that you can tap into the beta reader teams of both authors. This not only expands the pool of people available to provide input (and, ideally, eventually to provide positive reviews), but also serves as an early test of how much cross-pollination of your reader bases you can expect. If one author's beta readers love the coauthored work and the other's authors readers are lukewarm, you can factor this into your marketing and promotion plans.

Engaging Editorial Pros - Editors and Proofreaders

Engaging an editor brings both editorial expertise and an impartial, third-party perspective to your work. In coauthoring, you gain some flexibility, since each author can bring a degree of objectivity to the other's contributions. If both authors are deeply experienced in the topic, you might choose to rely on trusted peers from your beta reader pool for feedback instead.

Advances in spelling and grammar tools built into writing apps—supplemented by add-ons like ProWritingAid, Grammarly, PerfectIt, and eagle-eyed beta readers may eliminate the need to pay for proofreading services. If you and your coauthor are comfortable using AI tools, programs like ChatGPT and Claude can also help identify grammatical errors and typos during your final review.

However, even the most attentive coauthors can have blind spots about the work, and beta readers won't necessarily offer the same objectivity, experience, or insight as a professional editor. Base your decision on your needs and budget—ideally having anticipated this conversation during your alignment discussions with your coauthor.

For Your Consideration

Consider the following and capture your responses in the downloadable document available at TheIndyAuthor.com/Collaborate. For this section ...

- Do you and/or your coauthor have an existing beta reader team who would be appropriate for your coauthored work? If not, how will you go about soliciting beta readers?

- Do you anticipate that you will hire a professional editor? If yes, which of you will act as the liaison to the editor?
- What tools (or other resources) will you use to ensure your work is free of grammatical errors and typos?

DESIGN: INTERIOR AND COVER

Interior

We strongly recommend that if your book is text-centric (versus, for example, a coffee table photography book) you do your own interior formatting to create the files needed for your ebook and print editions. You'll quickly earn back the relatively low cost of tools that will easily produce the needed ebook and print book interior files through the savings of not having to pay someone else to do this for you. Furthermore, having access to these tools means that updates such as corrections to typos or updated Also By lists in the back matter are easy to make, making your content high quality and up to date. As of this writing, two popular options for interior formatting are the Mac-based Vellum and the web-based Atticus.

If you have more image-centric work or unique formatting needs, Adobe InDesign is the gold standard for advanced interior formatting, but it has a steep learning curve. Unless you or your coauthor are in a position to take on this work, hiring an expert might make more sense in this case. Be sure to discuss this with your collaborator in your alignment discussion.

We don't recommend using Microsoft Word for formatting, because the process is cumbersome and error-prone, and the results are often suboptimal; you'll spend more time and effort creating an inferior product.

Cover Design

When we decided to collaborate on *From Page to Platform*, Matty, under whose imprint the book would be published, already had two nonfiction books with professionally designed covers. These provided a design template, setting a standard for design elements like positioning of elements; general color scheme; and font selections for the title, subtitle, author name, and back cover text. By building from this template, Matty was able to create the covers for *From Page to Platform* and *Collaborate to Create* in Canva (although there were still issues to deal with that wouldn't have arisen if we had hired a cover design pro, such as adjustments needed to the positioning of the back cover text).

If you don't have a professionally designed template to base your cover design on, hire a pro. The result will be more polished, and outsourcing this work will enable you and your coauthor to focus on the part of the book that only the two of you can do: writing. Keeping the design simple—which usually works well for a nonfiction book—will help keep down costs.

Even if you hire a pro, it can be both fun and useful to create a mockup yourself. (You might use this cover for your advance reader ebook copies.) This can be a great way to align on a general direction with your coauthor before you engage a designer. Your pre-contract alignment discussions will ensure you have a common understanding of the approximate cost of the pro design and the responsibilities for coordinating the work.

We'd be remiss if we didn't mention AI for cover art. The astounding capabilities of AI-created art make it a viable option in some circumstances; the technology is improving so rapidly that any advice we provide on that front would be out of date months, if not weeks, after the publication of this book. However, consider that, at least of the time of this writing, AI art is still usually identifiable as AI art, and you may turn off potential buyers with an AI-generated cover. Also at the time of this writing, AI art is not copyrightable, so you risk having your cover art appear elsewhere, with no legal recourse. Research the current state of AI art and applicable copyright laws in effect at the time of your book's publication.

For Your Consideration

Consider the following and capture your responses in the downloadable document available at TheIndyAuthor.com/Collaborate. For this section ...

- What tools or resources will you use for interior design, and who will coordinate that work?
- What tools or resource will you use for cover design, and who will coordinate that work?

PRODUCTION AND DISTRIBUTION

You now have a properly formatted book with a cover that fits your target market. Next, you and your coauthor must decide where to publish your book and how to distribute it.

Entire books can be—and have been—written on recommended approaches to and best practices for book production and distribution, so in this section we'll give a brief description of the approach we have used for our coauthored books and our reasons for choosing that approach.

Formats

There are three primary formats in which books are published—ebook, print, and audio—and we recommend publishing your book at the very least in ebook and print.

Ebooks

Ebooks are ubiquitous. They are easy to format and produce and are hugely popular. Many readers prefer to read on e-readers, tablets, and phones. Making your book available as an ebook is non-negotiable.

Print

Indie authors can add a print edition to their offerings for very little incremental effort, especially if you're using an interior design and formatting tool like Vellum or Atticus. Too many authors overlook the benefits of the availability of a print edition, but print continues to retain a significant share of the market, and the benefits of print for nonfiction are especially clear when the book is one that a reader might want to pick up from their bookshelf for quick reference.

There are two methods for producing print editions: off-set printing and print on-demand (POD).

- With off-set printing, you pay upfront for a print run of at least several hundred copies, and you hold and manage the inventory.
- With POD, your book is printed when an order is placed for it. You don't need to keep any copies on hand, and sales and fulfillment are handled by the distributor.

We recommend starting with print on demand and only consider off-set printing if your book is successful and you feel that the benefits of a print run outweigh its downsides.

You should also assess the various print options: paperback, hardcover, and large print. We recommend you always offer a regular print paperback edition and perhaps wait to assess the potential audience for hardcover and large print. (Note that you will need to have separate cover designs for each of these options.)

Audio

Audio is an increasingly popular format, but producing an audiobook is definitely more of an investment in time, money, or both. Let's look at the two broad categories of audio: human-narrated and AI-narrated.

With human-narrated audiobooks, you pay a professional narrator to voice your book to life and generally pay them either through a per finished hour rate (in other words, you pay based on how long the finished audiobook is, not on how long it took them to produce it) or on a royalty share basis.

Human-narrated audiobooks can be sold on Audible, Spotify, and a number of other audiobook retailers. You can use a distributor like Findaway Voices to maximize your audiobook distribution.

High-quality human-narrated audio is time-consuming to create and therefore expensive to produce. For this reason, we recommend human-narrated audiobooks only if your book sales can fund it, or if creating an audiobook is truly a passion for you and your coauthor.

AI-narrated audiobooks aim to create a lifelike experience that mimics human-narrated audiobooks. The quality of these recordings used to be somewhat laughable, but no one is laughing now; the quality is improving exponentially. At some point, readers may not be able to distinguish between AI and human narrators. (In fact, options are available that would enable a favorite human narrator to train an AI on their voice, so that a series, for example, could be narrated by a combination of human and human-trained AI and these would be indistinguishable from each other.)

We believe that AI-narrated audio is especially appealing for nonfiction, where listeners may be looking more for a convenient way to consume the content than for a performance of the material as they might for a fiction work. We created AI-narrated audio for *From Page to Platform* using Google Play, which doesn't preclude us from later choosing to create a premium audiobook edition that we might narrate ourselves, or with AIs trained on our own voices.

Note that AI narration is not accepted on all retail distribution platforms at this time; to research the status at the time of your books' publication, search online for *distribution and retail platforms accepting AI-narrated audiobooks.* (Direct sales on your own online store is always an option.)

Wide or Exclusive

Another production / distribution decision you will need to make is whether to "go wide or exclusive." Going exclusive generally refers to making an ebook or audio exclusive on Amazon through their KDP Select / Kindle Unlimited program (for ebooks) or Amazon ACX (for audio, which distributes to Amazon, Audible, and iTunes). Going wide means making the book available on multiple platforms. (Note that exclusivity does not apply to print.)

We wholeheartedly recommend going wide. We believe that putting all your IP eggs in one retail basket is never a good idea, especially for nonfiction books; the authors who have found success in Amazon's exclusive KDP Select / Kindle Unlimited programs are almost always authors of specific fiction genres, including romance and fantasy. Distribution beyond Amazon also makes your book far more attractive to bookstores and libraries. And you can cut out the middleman entirely by selling direct from your own online store, perhaps on your website or via a platform like Shopify or PayHip.

Serve the whole pool of your potential readers by making your book available on as many retail platforms as reasonably possible (more on that in a moment). If you'd like more information about wide distribution, check out Mark Leslie Lefebvre's book *Wide for the Win.*

Direct or via an Aggregator

If you decide to "go wide," another decision you and your collaborator will need to make is whether to go to each retail or distribution platform directly or to use an aggregator. A simplified way of looking at this is which you value more: money or time.

Loading your books directly to a retail or distribution platform—for example, Amazon, Apple, Barnes & Noble, Google Play, and Kobo, to name just a few—favors money. It results in the highest per unit royalties because there is no middleman between you and the platform. The downside is that you need to manage each of these platforms individually: uploading interior and exterior files, entering and maintaining metadata, adjusting pricing, and so on. This would be extraordinarily time-consuming to do for all these platforms, leading to the phrase "death by dashboard."

Loading your books to all retail or distribution platforms via an aggregator—for example, Draft2Digital—favors time. For a cut of the proceeds, usually about 10%, you load your books and the associated data to one platform, which then sends it out to the selected distribution and retail platforms. The downside of this approach is not only the cut of the royalties you give up, but also that you lose some platform-specific flexibility, such as designating launch dates or participating in platform-specific promotions.

Our recommended approach, at least for authors earlier in their publishing careers, is to:

- go direct to Amazon via KDP for ebook and print (and via Amazon ACX for audio, if applicable); and
- go via an aggregator like Draft2Digital for ebook

and IngramSpark for print (and Findaway Voice for
audio) for other platforms.

As you become more familiar with the various options, you
can expand the platforms to which you go direct; for example,
Matty originally distributed to Kobo via Draft2Digital but eventually moved to going direct to Kobo via its Kobo Writing Life
platform to make better use of its promotional opportunities.

This is a severely simplified view of book production and
distribution; for more information, check out the resources from
the Alliance of Independent Authors at:

https://www.allianceindependentauthors.org/
https://selfpublishingadvice.org/

For Your Consideration

Consider the following and capture your responses in the downloadable document available at TheIndyAuthor.com/Collabo
rate. For this section …

- In what formats (ebook, print, audio) will you
  produce and distribute your books? Will some
  formats be available immediately while others might
  come later?
- Will you choose wide or exclusive distribution of
  your ebooks and, if applicable, audio?
- If wide, will you go direct or use an aggregator? If
  you plan to use a combination approach, to which
  platforms will you go direct?

MARKETING

By marketing, we mean those ongoing activities you engage in to stay in touch with your fans and followers, current and potential. It's the hand you extend to introduce yourself to readers, and how you position yourself in the marketplace. Marketing activities are ongoing (versus promotional activities, which are time-bound).

Pricing

We start out with pricing because the price you set for your book is a decision that straddles production and marketing (and, in fact, promotion). Each format you create (ebook, print, and audio) has its own unique pricing considerations.

For example, from a production point of view, you need to set your print book price high enough that you will still earn a reasonable royalty after production costs are deducted. You will also need to decide whether to offer a trade discount and whether you will accept returns—both of which will make the book more appealing to bookstores, but which will eat into your profits.

Ebook pricing has its own considerations. For example, the price you set for your book can affect the royalty rate you receive. At the time of this writing, indie authors in the U.S. receive higher royalties on Amazon for books priced between $2.99 and $9.99 than for books priced outside that range.

From a marketing point of view, you need to ensure that your price is hitting the right balance between being high enough to provide you with reasonable revenue per sale and low enough not to price yourself out of reach of your target readership. To determine the best starting point, research the price of other books (1) in your genre and (2) by authors of a similar standing (the top experts in your topic area can command more for their books than a lesser-known author). Note that nonfiction books usually command a higher price than fiction books of a similar length.

Ensure that your regular price is high enough that you have room for discounting (discussed later). If the regular price for your ebook is $1.99—which we don't recommend—then a discount to $0.99 isn't very attention-getting.

Note especially for indie authors: there is as much danger in pricing your book too low as in pricing it too high. You are writing your book to bring value to your readers; make sure the price you ask for it reflects that. No one benefits from a "race to the bottom" with price.

The Triumvirate of Marketing: Email Newsletter, Website, and Other Online Presence

The other aspects of marketing are often focused just as much on an author as on a book, which makes marketing one of the areas that's easiest to overlook for a coauthored book ... and sometimes the trickiest to negotiate.

Another aspect that makes marketing a coauthored book

especially challenging is that marketing is not time-bound; you should still be adhering to some marketing plan years after the launch of your book. Who will have responsibility for ensuring that the book has a marketing presence for as long as it makes business sense?

For solo works, marketing is usually based on the triumvirate of email newsletter, a website, and other online presence (such as social media). For all of these, we recommend that each of you don't try to spin up new, joint assets—for example, a shared email, a shared website, shared social media profiles—in support of your coauthored book; you'll reach your marketing goals much more easily and effectively by using the existing individual assets you might have. (An exception might be if both of you want to use your book as a calling card to other offerings such as joint speaking engagements, jointly conducted classes, or joint consulting, but that is more like a full business partnership than the production of a single coauthored work and is beyond the scope of this book.)

However, you do need to coordinate how you will use your individual assets in support of your collaborative work. Factor in considerations such as:

- Will one person create content that can be used by both authors?
- How often will you include mention of your book in your individual newsletters?
- How will you represent the book on each of your websites? Should the look and feel of the presentation be consistent with the website it appears on, or consistent across both websites?
- How will you represent your book on social media? Who will take responsibility for creating assets with images and copy? On what social media platforms

will you have a presence? Who will take the lead on each platform?

Managing Real-time and In-person Events

Author appearances could also be considered marketing activities. Agree on whether both authors will need to participate in opportunities like podcast interviews or blog posts. We recommend that joint participation not be a requirement since coordinating with the event host and both authors poses logistical difficulties. If each author brings different knowledge to the coauthored work, then each author can pitch themselves with a focus on their area of expertise. For example, in Matty's coauthored book with Mark Lefebvre, *Taking the Short Tack*, Matty's expertise is in indie-published short fiction, so if Matty is conducting a podcast interview about *Taking the Short Tack*, she focuses her discussion on the indie angle.

If your marketing plan includes in-person author events and you and your coauthor don't live close together, discuss how you will handle these—for example, will you make an attempt to involve a geographically distant coauthor in in-person events via a virtual meeting app?

Consider what supporting materials might be useful for your author events to make sure you and your collaborator are in sync on the messages you want to be conveying. For example, you might create a high-level list of talking points for podcast guest appearances or interviews.

If a marketing event or activity carries a cost, decide on if and how you will share those expenses. We recommend using a 50-50 split for all marketing expenses, but you and your coauthor can discuss each expense as it comes up and how to account for it. Will you reimburse each other monthly? Quarterly? When a discrepancy hits a certain dollar amount threshold?

For Your Consideration

Consider the following and capture your responses in the downloadable document available at TheIndyAuthor.com/Collaborate. For this section ...

- What will be the price of your book for each format?
- How will you coordinate marketing activities across the triumvirate of email newsletters, websites, and online platforms like social media?
- How will you coordinate participation in real-time and in-person events?
- How will you ensure that marketing occurs appropriately over time (perhaps years after the publication of the book)?

PROMOTION

Whereas marketing refers to the ongoing activities to position yourself and your books in the marketplace, promotion involves the time-specific activities targeted at selling books—for example, price discounts. By the time your work is ready to launch, promotion will be one of your priorities, and being aligned with your coauthor on your plans in this area smooths the way to efficient and effective promotion.

An entire library of books could be (and has been) written about promotion, but here are some high-level considerations to discuss with your coauthor.

- **Assign a promotion lead.** The promotion lead is responsible for ensuring adherence to the promotion strategy, and for ensuring that the collaborators re-assess that strategy periodically. It is not—or at least not necessarily—the person who will execute all the promotion activities.
- **Agree on how promotional activities will be funded.** 50/50 usually makes sense.

- **Agree on promotion platforms.** On what platforms (Amazon, BookBub, Facebook, etc.) will you promote your book? This is an area where dividing and conquering can be helpful. If one of you is more familiar with Amazon ads and another is more familiar with Facebook ads, you can capitalize on your areas of expertise while still adhering to an overall promotion strategy as monitored by the promotion lead. Maintain a list of ideas both collaborators can contribute to as ideas arise for places the book can be promoted.
- **Agree on a promotion strategy**, including:
  - the amount you and your coauthor want to spend on promotions—either a flat fee, to be revisited based on book sales, or a percentage of sales
  - the overall schedule—for example, heavy promotion across a suite of promotion platforms around the book's launch followed by a rotating schedule of promotions, each focusing on one platform, and some ongoing promotion on key retail platforms (for example, Amazon ads)
- **Create a promotion calendar.** The promotion lead should maintain a calendar of promo activities; this will help avoid a situation where, for example, one author pitches the book to a promo platform at a $2.99 sale price while the other author pitches it at the same time at a $0.99 sale price. And speaking of pricing ...

Pricing

Just as pricing factors into production and marketing, it factors into promotion as well, specifically related to discounting your regular price for promotional activities.

For many years, discounting an ebook almost always meant setting a sale price of $0.99, but now books on promotion platforms like BookBub are often $1.99 or even $2.99.

You and your collaborator should experiment with different sales prices to determine what price and promotional approach best meets your business goals.

Ratings and Reviews

Since so many readers use ratings and reviews to help sift through the enormous selection of books available on any topic, a pool of positive reader reviews is a great asset to have to promote your books. A few quick notes about ratings and reviews ...

More is better than perfect. If readers see that your book has five five-star reviews on a retail platform, they will assume (probably correctly) that those reviews came from friends and family, and they will be likely to discount them. However, if they see that your book has 25 ratings with an average rating of four stars, they will ascribe greater weight to those reviews.

So how do you get those reviews? Consider that there are two types: editorial and reader reviews.

Editorial Reviews

There are some legitimate and reputable platforms which you can pay for a review; the best-known is Kirkus Reviews. Kirkus is a desirable platform because paying for a review does not guarantee a positive review, and so a good review from Kirkus is taken seriously. It can be a risky platform because you might end up paying for a negative review, and your only recourse is to ask Kirkus not to publish the review.

Neither Matty nor Michael has ever requested a Kirkus Review for a nonfiction book; we rely on our circle of writing and publishing colleagues to provide these types of "trade reviews" (although Matty has used Kirkus for her fiction and continues to use those positive reviews in her promotional activities).

Reader Reviews

You can also ask readers for reviews directly, either by offering advance review copies or asking for reviews in the back of your book. This is a great way to gather organic reviews.

You can also reach out to book bloggers and influencers to see if they would be willing to read your book in exchange for a review.

A paid option is to use a platform that serves as a match-maker between books and readers who enjoy writing reviews. In this case, you are paying for the service the platform provides—hosting copies of your book that reader / reviewers can download for free, facilitating the process of leaving reviews, providing tracking of reviewer activities, etc. As with Kirkus, authors are not paying for good reviews; you are paying for the facilitative service. The pool of services available changes over time, so do an online search for *best book review sites for authors* and the current year to see what's available, and of course check these against the Alliance of Independent Authors ratings service: https://selfpublishingadvice.org/ratings

The key message here is that you should never pay for reader reviews themselves; this is unethical and violates the terms of most retail platforms. This is different from paying for services that facilitate the review process—such as distributing advance copies or connecting with potential reviewers—as long as there's no guarantee of a review or of a positive outcome.

For Your Consideration

Consider the following and capture your responses in the downloadable document available at TheIndyAuthor.com/Collaborate. For this section ...

- Who will serve as the promotion lead?
- What are the comparable books (in your genre and written by authors of a similar status) you will use to determine your price?
- What will the price of your book be on all available formats (ebook, paperback, hardcover, large print, etc.)?
- What strategy and platforms will you use to get reviews?

NEGOTIATING THE PROCESS

By the time you embark on your collaborative project, you and your coauthor will have laid the foundation for success by aligning on expectations and will have formalized the partnership with a contract. But no matter how careful your pre-collaboration planning is, you can't foresee every possible question or issue that will arise during the project. In this section, we'll share some recommendations for how to negotiate your interactions with your coauthor not only to produce your best work, but to make the process as enjoyable as possible for both of you. Below are some aspects of the project that might require negotiation.

Scope / Word Count

What if you or your collaborator wants to change the agreed-upon scope or word count of the project? Our recommendations differ depending on whether the proposed changes are an expansion or a reduction of the agreed-upon scope or word count.

For example, if you have agreed that the work will be about

50K words and as you collect content you find that you have 75K words worth of material, it makes sense to reduce your scope to come in closer to the 50K word target. The reason for this is that the length of the work is a good barometer of the effort you and your collaborator will put into it. If you've allocated time in your schedule to complete your part of a 50K-word book, it will require replanning for you to accommodate the time needed to complete your part of a 75K-word book. And if material gets left out of the current work in progress, it could be fodder for a future collaboration!

We originally intended *Collaborate to Create* to address both nonfiction and fiction, but as we began the work to conceptualize and frame out the book, we realized that the processes were different enough that it would result in a book about twice as long as our agreed-upon word count. We decided to focus on nonfiction, with a book on coauthoring fiction as a possible future collaborative work.

On the other hand, if you and your coauthor have agreed that the work will be about 50K words and you find you have 35K worth of material, and you feel that a 35K-word book will not be appealing to your target audience, then you may need to expand the scope of the content you address ... assuming, of course, that it makes sense.

The trickiest situation might be when the amount of content seems right for the length of the work you want to produce, but you or your collaborator wants to, say, double the scope and the length of the work. Here we recommend that you stick with your initial agreement since it reflects the time and effort you have set aside for your coauthored project.

Content

The type of content you create for your book will be guided at a high level by your pre-contract alignment. However, the detail of that content will need to be negotiated throughout the process. Much of this negotiation will be trivial and often resolved without issue. For example, for our coauthored book *From Page to Platform*, Matty was interested in including information on author readings, and Michael was happy to have the book include that as long as Matty drafted that material.

However, there will be times when you arrive at an impasse.

For example, neither of us feels comfortable advising writers to do something that we ourselves don't do, so we had to do a bit of negotiation regarding one piece of advice for "The Speaker on the Road" in *From Page to Platform*. Michael felt strongly about including an unequivocal recommendation for readers to purchase travel insurance. Matty, on the other hand, didn't feel comfortable attaching her name to that recommendation; it wasn't because she thought travel insurance was a bad idea, but because she generally didn't purchase it herself and didn't want to attach her name to a recommendation she herself didn't act on. The issue was easily resolved by including a note in the book that that particular recommendation came specifically from Michael.

But what if your coauthor wants to include information with which you actively disagree? Both of your names will be on the cover, so it's reasonable for a reader to assume that its contents represents both its creators' perspectives, and it's probably not appropriate for you and your collaborator to document your disagreement on the page.

One option is to leave the information out. But this should be a last resort, not a first resort, because it sets a dangerous precedent and risks gutting the book of its value.

Is the disagreement over the accuracy of factual data? Look for an authoritative source to confirm or refute the information.

Is the disagreement over a piece of content's applicability to your topic or appropriateness for your target audience? Revisit your alignment document for previous agreements against which to measure the material. Consider—or encourage your coauthor to consider—whether the person lobbying for inclusion of the content could use it elsewhere than the coauthored work.

In the section on "Aligning on Expectations," we recommend you agree on who has the final say in decisions about various aspects of the project, and this should include matters of content. We have a clause in our contract that specifies that Matty, as the publisher of the work, has final say in all issues. However, it's hard for us to imagine actually invoking that clause. First, our general alignment on our strategic direction and goals makes that scenario unlikely. Second, such an action would undoubtedly undermine our professional relationship. Invoke such an agreement with caution. Ask yourself whether a particular issue is the hill you're willing to die on. Strictly speaking, you can only die on a hill once—then you're dead. Choose your positions accordingly.

The Creative Process

There is perhaps nothing that feels more personal and therefore more vulnerable to a writer than their writing. In a coauthored work, the writing has to be less personal, since it doesn't belong to you alone, while also feeling even more vulnerable, since you must expose it to the creative process of another person. As author Todd Harra says:

> *Tensions can run higher in something like this than in a standard business transaction because you've got a little piece of your soul attached to the work, and you've got two people that are emotionally invested in it. Things can happen.*

The process of coauthorship is one that could have been a minefield for us, because we have very different creative processes. Michael describes himself as a "first draft final (sort of) writer," whereas the iterative process described in the section on "Creating the Content" is much more reflective of Matty's approach for both collaborative and solo work.

However, this never proved to be an issue. We had the benefit of having a solid professional relationship before we embarked on our first collaboration, *From Page to Platform*. We also checked in with each other throughout the drafting and editing process. Here's an email Michael sent to Matty:

Matty, I reviewed your chapters today and provided my comments. Please let me know if the feedback was helpful or if it was too disruptive—I don't want to interfere with your creative process. Moving forward, I'm happy to save my feedback until you are ready for it if that will be more helpful to you—just let me know what you prefer. Sometimes I can get overzealous with comments. If I don't comment, I will forget it. :) With me, you are always welcome to comment.

There was no issue. From Matty's point of view, Michael's input was thoughtfully presented without being overly delicate (which risks having the recipient of the input miss the point).

From Michael's perspective, Matty did a great job of proposing a phone call for more complex topics that were too difficult to discuss in a comment on the Word document. Also, because we have regular communication, we both felt empowered to bring up issues we were facing in the manuscript during those communications.

Here are some guidelines about smoothing the way to exchanging editorial input with your collaborator:

- **Specify the preferred venue.** Do you prefer to hear or to read any input your coauthor has for you? When you're providing input, do you prefer to talk it out or write it out?
- **Specify the preferred time.** We may be pretty brave about receiving input on our work most of the time, but if we've just had a terrible day at work or an argument with our spouse or a fender bender in the grocery store parking lot, we may not be in the best frame of mind to hear critique in a productive way. Ask your coauthor for permission before you provide input, and feel free to ask your coauthor to postpone providing input if you are in a particularly sensitive frame of mind. (But keep in mind you'll need to hear the input at some point, so don't use this excuse excessively.)
- **Reserve your response.** This can be a benefit of getting input in writing rather than in person; it makes immediate response slightly more difficult. Give yourself time to consider your coauthor's input and weigh its value with the additional objectivity that time can provide.

For more tips, check out Episode 88 of *The Indy Author Podcast*: "How to Receive and Give Critique with Tiffany Yates Martin."

Dealing with Imposter Syndrome

It's likely that at some point in a collaboration, even the most confident author will find themselves facing imposter syndrome.

Here's Matty's experience:

When I coauthored Taking the Short Tack *with Mark Leslie Lefebvre, the moment of imposter syndrome came for me when I started realizing how narrow my experience with the short fiction market was in comparison to Mark's, and how much I was relying on him for the content for many of the topics. Over the course of the project, however, I realized that where Mark was providing the raw materials, I was providing more editorial work as well as most of the production and distribution work, and so the overall effort seemed equitable.*

When I coauthored From Page to Platform *with Michael, one of the most productive authors I know, imposter syndrome struck every time I saw that Michael had contributed a thousand words for every hundred I had contributed. This feeling was completely self-inflicted; Michael never made me feel guilty for not being able to keep up with his astounding productivity. In fact, one of the drivers behind* Collaborate to Create *was the belief that I could do the "heavy lifting" of content creation for this book and pay Michael back for the disproportionate amount of work he had done on the earlier book.*

Here is Michael's experience:

Everybody deals with imposter syndrome in their own way. You'll find that things trigger it for no reason. But the truth is that because everyone deals with imposter syndrome, no one is an imposter. And if you think about it, a true imposter wouldn't be thinking so hard about why they don't belong—they'd be using their powers for evil.

Imposter syndrome is a sign that you're doing things right. You're second-guessing yourself because you care. When you coauthor a book, you're creating something that neither you nor the coauthor could create on their own. You both bring your respective talents to the table. If it weren't for those talents, you wouldn't be working together! Keep that in perspective the next time imposter syndrome knocks at your door.

For Your Consideration

Consider the following and capture your responses in the downloadable document available at TheIndyAuthor.com/Collaborate. For this section ...

Capture the agreement you and your coauthor have about:

- Negotiating changes to scope?
- Providing feedback on content?
- How (via conversation or in writing) and when will it be best for each collaborator to receive input from their creative partner?

IT'S NOT JUST THE BOOK

The focus of your collaborative effort will be your coauthored book, but you have the opportunity to expand the value you can bring to those interested in your topic beyond the book. Looking beyond the book can also increase the value your work can bring to you and your collaborator. In the same way that *multiple streams of income* has become a by-word within the author community, so *intellectual property* or IP is becoming a by-word for how to maximize the value of your work.

Workbook / Worksheet

This might include checklists, templates, cheat sheets, quick reference guides, case studies, or bonus content. An example of this would be the downloadable "For Your Consideration" worksheet we reference at the end of each section; this document not only provides added value to readers of the book but also entices people who have not yet bought the book to check it out. More robust workbooks can even be sold as separate, revenue-generating offerings.

Presentations

Especially for nonfiction books, co-presenting on the topic of your book is a great way to market your book and to capitalize on opportunities like building your community and expanding your audience reach. Speaking opportunities may come with speaker fees, adding another revenue stream from your shared IP. Discuss up-front if and how you and your collaborator will share this income.

You can use an iterative process similar to the process we describe in the section on "Creating the Content" for your presentation, but once the presentation is largely finalized, one person should maintain the master, with the other collaborator funneling any requests for changes to the owner. An exception to this might be if you and your collaborator have very different presentation styles—for example, one likes to use bulleted slides while the other prefers images. In this case, you might each keep your own version of the presentation. However, always ensure that the message each of you is delivering is aligned.

When developing the presentation, mark individual slides with a subtle indicator about who should be addressing that slide. For example, we might put Matty's The Indy Author logo on slides she will address and Michael's Author Level Up logo on slides he will address.

Agree on roughly how much time should be spent on each slide and find a way to mark it subtly on the slide or in the notes. The reason we recommend this is that it's much more difficult to adjust the pace of a presentation with two presenters than with one presenter, and this tip helps ensure that the presentation as a whole comes in at or near the target duration.

If you create your slides in PowerPoint, don't share that file on Google Drive and expect to use it for anything other than a rough reference copy; the format, layout, and fonts will not necessarily be retained. Have one collaborator maintain a master in the native format locally and share it with the other collaborator as needed.

For each presentation opportunity, agree on the extent to which the non-primary presenter should interject when their coauthor is the primary presenter. For example, should the non-primary presenter raise their hand and wait to be recognized by the presenter? Should they feel free to interject comments in a more informal way? There are no right or wrong approaches as long as you and your co-presenter agree on how to handle the situation.

And to make sure each presentation opportunity goes smoothly, assign one person to coordinate with each event organizer.

You'll find lots more best practices for presentations in our coauthored book *From Page to Platform: How to Succeed as an Author Speaker*.

Slicing and Dicing

Consider other IP that you can create from your book. For example, some of the chapters in our coauthored *From Page to Platform* could function as standalone topics, so we could pitch those as articles to publications as long as the publisher knew the material was excerpted from a longer work and as long is its use didn't limit our own use of that material in the book.

For Your Consideration

Consider the following and capture your responses in the down-loadable document available at TheIndyAuthor.com/Collabo rate. For this section ...

- What companion offerings might you want to offer along with your book to bring maximum value to your readers and to capitalize on your joint IP beyond the book?

IT'S NEVER OVER

The Care and Feeding of Your Collaborative Relationship

One of the beauties of being an independently published author is that you control your copyright for your entire life plus many, many years after you die. In the United States, copyright control lasts for the author's life plus seventy years. Most countries around the world have similar laws.

This is both a benefit and a challenge when the IP is co-created. In order to continue to enjoy the benefits of your co-created IP, you and your coauthor will need to continue to manage your rights proactively, establish clear agreements about ownership and decision-making, and put a plan in place for how the IP will be handled after one or both of you are gone.

On the other hand, it's possible that you and your collaborator had a specific goal for the book that was met when it was published—for example, to pave the way for speaking engagements on the topic. You might agree that you're willing to sacrifice the potential for additional sales in order to save the time on the promotion activities that would trigger those sales. Any goal is valid as long as you and your coauthor have agreed to it upfront.

It's possible, of course, that your goals for the book evolve over time. For example, you both might go into the collaboration thinking that you want the book as a calling card for speaking engagements, but over time one of you begins to be more interested in income from sales where the other one is not. Even this scenario is negotiable—the person looking for income might agree to take on the time and expense of promotion in exchange for a larger percentage of the royalties. Again, coming to an updated common understanding is the key to the ongoing success of the relationship.

The most successful coauthoring relationships aren't built only on alignment on shared goals at the outset, but on a willingness to communicate, adapt, and support each other over time.

What to Do if Things Go Bad

If you've followed the advice in this book, the chances of your coauthored project going bad will be greatly reduced, but no advice can reduce that risk to zero. In this section, we examine a few possible challenges and share advice for addressing them.

What if your coauthor has gone radio-silent?

- Try another means of communication – If you normally use email, try giving them a call or sending a message through a different platform.
- Give them time to reply – They may be on vacation, dealing with a personal emergency, or simply overwhelmed. Set a reasonable timeframe before assuming the worst.
- Check for recent activity – If your coauthor is active on social media or engaging in other professional

activities but hasn't responded to you, it may indicate a lack of interest in the project, shifting priorities, or an intentional avoidance of communication. If this seems to be the case, consider reaching out with a direct but non-confrontational message to clarify their level of commitment.

- Express your concerns clearly – If the delay continues, send a polite but direct message outlining your concerns and asking for an update on their availability.
- Refer to your agreement – If you have a coauthoring contract or written agreement, revisit it to determine the next steps if one party becomes unresponsive.
- Decide on a path forward – If repeated attempts to connect go unanswered, you may need to consider steps such as pausing the project, seeking mediation, or, in extreme cases, legal intervention to determine rights and responsibilities.

What if your coauthor is not executing on their responsibilities?

- Clarify expectations – Revisit your alignment document and contract, as well as any other supporting documents such as project plans or task lists. Are deadlines and tasks clearly defined? If expectations were vague, a simple clarification might resolve the issue.
- Check for obstacles – Your coauthor may be dealing with personal or professional challenges that are affecting their ability to contribute. Have an open

conversation to see if they need support or
adjustments to the workload.

- Reiterate the impact on the project – Frame your
concerns around the shared goals of the book rather
than assigning blame. A message like, "I want to
make sure we stay on track—how can we adjust
things to move forward?" can encourage
collaboration rather than defensiveness.
- Offer solutions – If they're struggling with certain
tasks, discuss whether you can redistribute
responsibilities, bring in outside help, or adjust
deadlines to keep progress steady.
- Refer to your agreement – If necessary, remind your
coauthor of any written agreements regarding roles,
responsibilities, and expectations for completing the
project.
- Set a deadline for resolution – If delays continue,
establish a firm but fair timeline for action. Let them
know that if they can't meet their commitments,
you'll need to explore alternatives, such as
completing the book yourself or engaging another
contributor.
- Decide on next steps – If the situation doesn't
improve, consider whether you need to renegotiate
terms, reassign work, or even dissolve the
partnership if it's no longer productive. Review your
contract for options for modifying or terminating
the agreement if necessary.

Extracting Yourself from an In-Process Collaboration

If you've exhausted your options for how to remedy a relationship that has gone bad, you'll need to consider your legal

options, ideally based on the contract you and your collaborator signed. The Alliance of Independent Authors and Writer Beware can be good resources to help you decide what your best next steps are. While these organizations cannot mediate your dispute, they may have helpful resources to guide you.

What if your partnership has shifted to another person?

You might have an excellent relationship with your collaborator, but if they pass away, you will be dealing with their heirs—people you likely have a much more tenuous relationship with. Michael likes to say that when you coauthor a book with someone, you're also entering into a business agreement with their spouse and heirs. If your coauthor dies, you will have to work with their heirs on royalties, licensing opportunities, and the general management and maintenance of the book. Do they prefer to be hands on? Hands off? It's a minor detail now, but something to at least discuss briefly with your coauthor.

If the spouse or heirs would prefer you to handle everything and just send them a check a couple times a year, that's worth knowing upfront. If the spouse and heirs want to more actively involved, that's also worth knowing. It's also important to point out that spouses and heirs might not even be thinking about this. We would recommend at least broaching the conversation and including your wishes in your estate plan so that this is on their radar. For more information about this, refer to Michael's books *The Author Estate Handbook* and *The Author Heir Handbook*.

For Your Consideration

Consider the following and capture your responses in the downloadable document available at TheIndyAuthor.com/Collaborate. For this section ...

- What is your plan if the collaboration doesn't go as planned? How will you resolve disputes? What will you do if you reach an impasse?
- What is your plan for when you or you coauthor passes away?

CONCLUSION: SETTING THE STAGE FOR FUTURE COLLABORATIONS

The advice we've shared in *Collaborate to Create* will pave the way to a successful coauthoring effort even if it's your first collaborative project, but each creative collaboration is unique, and by the end of that first effort, you will have learned what did and didn't work for you and your collaborator. You may be eager to continue building on the collaborative relationship you've established with your coauthor—and hopefully your coauthor feels the same way! Ideally, you can apply everything you've learned to more collaborations going forward.

When we neared the end of the process that resulted in our coauthored book *From Page to Platform*, Matty said to Michael, "I hope we have an opportunity to put all our learnings to practice in another project!" ... and a book on coauthoring was the perfect place to do it!

We learned how to work cohesively and quickly, and how to create a quality product. We carried these learnings into this book. We also expanded our network, learned key aspects of each other's marketing styles, and gained other knowledge that benefited both our coauthoring and solo careers. For example, Michael learned about Matty's "book of the month" promotion strategy, where she picks a book from her catalogue to promote each month, and adopted it in his own solo marketing efforts. Matty gained insights into the techniques that enable Michael's extraordinary productivity and was able to increase her own productivity as a result.

Harking back to the examples we introduced at the beginning of this book, just as with the double-handed competitive sailors or the gamers tag-teaming a level in a video game, we combined our forces, improved our skills, and expanded our reach by collaborating to create. We're confident you'll see similar benefits in your coauthoring relationship.

In fact, we'd love to hear from you about your experiences with collaboration and what lessons you'd like to share with your fellow writers. Drop us a note at matty@mattydalrymple.com or michael@authorlevelup.com.

Happy coauthoring!

LOOKING FOR A SPEAKER ON COLLABORATING TO CREATE NONFICTION?

Are you part of a group or organizing an event catering to an audience that would be interested in more information about collaborating to create nonfiction? Matty and Michael would love to join you for a presentation on the topic! Drop either of us a note at matty@mattydalrymple.com or michael@author levelup.com.

ACKNOWLEDGMENTS

We'd like to thank the authors who shared their perspectives on collaboration for this book:

Michael Bracken

Bruce Robert Coffin

Todd Harra

Nicholas Harvey

Mark Leslie Lefebvre

Dr. Katherine Ramsland

Lee Savino

Kevin Tumlinson

And thank you to eagle-eyed proofreader Mary Dalrymple for her help with the final polish.

ABOUT THE AUTHORS

Matty Dalrymple is the author of the Lizzy Ballard Thrillers and the Ann Kinnear Suspense Novels and Suspense Shorts. She also podcasts, writes, speaks, and consults on the writing craft and the publishing voyage as The Indy Author. Writer's Digest has including TheIndyAuthor.com on its list of 101 Best Websites for Writers for multiple years. Since 2016 she has hosted hundreds of episodes of The Indy Author Podcast. She is the author of nonfiction books for authors and her articles have appeared in *Writer's Digest* magazine and *Indie Author Magazine*. She serves as the Campaigns Manager for the Alliance of Independent Authors. You can find Matty's fiction at https://www.mattydalrymple.com/ and her resources for writers at https://www.theindyauthor.com/.

Michael La Ronn is the author of over 100 science fiction & fantasy books and self-help books for writers. He writes from the great plains of Iowa and has managed to write while raising a family, working a full-time job, and even attending law school classes in the evenings. Michael also runs the award-winning YouTube channel "Author Level Up," with over 50,000 subscribers and 2 million views. *Writer's Digest* voted the channel one of the "Best Resources for Writers" in 2020. You can find his fiction at www.michaellaronn.com and his videos and books for writers at www.authorlevelup.com.

ALSO BY MATTY DALRYMPLE

The Lizzy Ballard Thrillers

Rock Paper Scissors (Book 1)

Snakes and Ladders (Book 2)

The Iron Ring (Book 3)

Kill Box Checkmate (Book 3½)

Scare Card (Book 4)

Drawing Dead (Book 5)

The Lizzy Ballard Thrillers Ebook Box Set

The Ann Kinnear Suspense Novels

The Sense of Death (Book 1)

The Sense of Reckoning (Book 2)

The Falcon and the Owl (Book 3)

A Furnace for Your Foe (Book 4)

A Serpent's Tooth (Book 5)

Be with the Dead (Book 6)

The Ann Kinnear Suspense Novels Ebook Box Set - Books 1-3

The Ann Kinnear Suspense Shorts

All Deaths Endure

Close These Eyes

May Violets Spring

Ministers of Grace

Our Dancing Days

Sea of Troubles

ISBN-13: 978-1-959882-21-3 (Ebook)

ISBN-13: 978-1-959882-22-0 (Print)